Anuj Sharma

A Handbook to Develop
a Digital Handwriting Interface

Anchor Academic
Publishing

Sharma, Anuj: A Handbook to Develop a Digital Handwriting Interface, Hamburg,
Anchor Academic Publishing 2016

Buch-ISBN: 978-3-96067-035-3
PDF-eBook-ISBN: 978-3-96067-535-8
Druck/Herstellung: Anchor Academic Publishing, Hamburg, 2016

Bibliografische Information der Deutschen Nationalbibliothek:
Die Deutsche Nationalbibliothek verzeichnet diese Publikation in der Deutschen
Nationalbibliografie; detaillierte bibliografische Daten sind im Internet über
http://dnb.d-nb.de abrufbar.

Bibliographical Information of the German National Library:
The German National Library lists this publication in the German National Bibliography.
Detailed bibliographic data can be found at: http://dnb.d-nb.de

All rights reserved. This publication may not be reproduced, stored in a retrieval system
or transmitted, in any form or by any means, electronic, mechanical, photocopying,
recording or otherwise, without the prior permission of the publishers.

Das Werk einschließlich aller seiner Teile ist urheberrechtlich geschützt. Jede Verwertung
außerhalb der Grenzen des Urheberrechtsgesetzes ist ohne Zustimmung des Verlages
unzulässig und strafbar. Dies gilt insbesondere für Vervielfältigungen, Übersetzungen,
Mikroverfilmungen und die Einspeicherung und Bearbeitung in elektronischen Systemen.

Die Wiedergabe von Gebrauchsnamen, Handelsnamen, Warenbezeichnungen usw. in
diesem Werk berechtigt auch ohne besondere Kennzeichnung nicht zu der Annahme,
dass solche Namen im Sinne der Warenzeichen- und Markenschutz-Gesetzgebung als frei
zu betrachten wären und daher von jedermann benutzt werden dürften.

Die Informationen in diesem Werk wurden mit Sorgfalt erarbeitet. Dennoch können
Fehler nicht vollständig ausgeschlossen werden und die Diplomica Verlag GmbH, die
Autoren oder Übersetzer übernehmen keine juristische Verantwortung oder irgendeine
Haftung für evtl. verbliebene fehlerhafte Angaben und deren Folgen.

Alle Rechte vorbehalten

© Anchor Academic Publishing, Imprint der Diplomica Verlag GmbH
Hermannstal 119k, 22119 Hamburg
http://www.diplomica-verlag.de, Hamburg 2016
Printed in Germany

ACKNOWLEDGEMENTS

I am grateful to Panjab University, Chandigarh for all resources that helped me to learn and write this book. I acknowledge the devotion and efforts made from Dr. Kalpana for this book. She has always inspired me to work harder for this prestigious book throughout my development of this digital handwriting interface. She imparted a lot of guidance and introduction needed regarding this inter-disciplinary work. I am thankful to my family members for their support to complete this work. I am grateful to my parents, my wife and daughter for their patience and cooperation. I wish this book could help readers to achieve their purpose and impart knowledge.

OUTLINE OF THE BOOK

The prime purpose of this book is to educate readers for the development of a Digital Handwriting Interface (DHI) where the user may write with a digital pen. This book includes code in VC++.NET language. The developed DHI has been found useful in many applications as sketch drawing, handwriting recognizer after inclusion of recognizer files and collection of digital handwriting. The reader will find this book useful as it includes the entire source code in chapter forms.

Chapter 1 includes the introduction to digital handwriting mainly for Indic scripts where keyboards are not popular and their use is complex. Therefore, digital handwriting is very useful for Indic scripts writing. Also, this chapter introduce user about development process of digital handwriting recognizer. **Chapter 2** includes source code and introduction for DHI interface. This chapter includes information that how handwriting is stored in form of coordinates and could be verified. The required source files to do this step are given in chapter 2. **Chapter 3** includes preprocessing steps where digital handwriting strokes noise is removed. This mainly include size normalization of handwritten stroke, correcting slants of handwritten strokes and removing flicker in handwritten strokes. This chapter include source files for preprocessing. **Chapter 4** include graph based data where preprocessed handwritten strokes could be displayed for user information. This graph based data can be visualized for different phases of preprocessing. **Chapter 5** includes other files that help in development of DHI. These files mainly include file save options, dialog options for writing words, colour selection of digital pen, width of digital pen etc. The Chapter 6 include necessary classes definitions in form of header files for all the files discussed from Chapter 2 to Chapter 5. **Chapter 6** also includes necessary screenshots that how developed DHI works. The DHI has been found very useful in research work for handwriting recognition.

CONTENTS

Contents	Page nos.
CHAPTER 1: INTRODUCTION	1-14
CHAPTER 2: USER INTERFACE DEVELOPMENT	15-40
CHAPTER 3: PREPROCESSING DEVELOPMENT	41-68
CHAPTER 4: PREPROCESSING GRAPH INTERFACE	69-97
CHAPTER 5: MISCELLANEOUS FILES FOR INTERFACE	98-120
CHAPTER 6: HEADER FILES	121-154
TABLE OF REFERENCE	155-167

CHAPTER 1

INTRODUCTION

Since the inception of computers we are witnessing a great deal of research activities in the field of computer human interface. The input devices such as keyboard and mouse have limitations *vis-à-vis* input through natural handwriting. The natural handwriting is a very easy way of exchanging information between computers and human beings. Also, it is difficult to input data to computers for scripts Chinese and Japanese as these scripts have a large number of alphabets. It is also difficult to input data for computers for scripts like Devanagiri and Gurmukhi owing to their complex typing nature. Two quick and natural ways of communication between users and computers are inputting the data through handwritten documents and through speech. Speech recognition has limitations in noisy environment and especially where privacy of an individual is required. In present work, we have focused on the problem of handwriting recognition only. Variations in handwriting is one prominent problem and achieving high degree of accuracy is a tedious task. These variations are caused by different writing styles. Variation in handwriting among different writers occurs since each writer possesses own speed of writing, different styles, sizes or positions for characters or text. Variation in handwriting styles also exists within individual person's handwriting. This variation may take place due to: writing in various situations that may or may not be comfortable to writer; different moods of writer; style of writing same characters with different shapes in different situations or as a part of different words; using different kinds of hardware for handwriting.

Handwriting recognition is in research for over four decades and has attracted many researchers across the world. Researchers in this area have made great advances and reliability of online handwriting based devices have been increased. The presence of online handwriting recognition in devices like personal digital assistant or tablet PCs is a very useful feature. Today, these devices are in good demand and their usages have increased a lot in recent past. The presence of online handwriting recognizer for Devanagiri, Gurmukhi, Bangla and other asian scripts shall provide a natural way of communication between users and computers and it will increase the usage of personal digital assistant or tablet PCs in indian languages. Also, some of the Asian scripts such as Devanagiri, Gurmukhi, Bangla and Tamil share many similarities and therefore advances made for one script with respect to online handwriting recognition could be useful for other such similar scripts.

1.1 ISSUES IN ONLINE HANDWRITING RECOGNITION SYSTEMS

The technique by which a computer system can recognize characters and other symbols written by hand in natural handwriting is called handwriting recognition system. Handwriting recognition is classified into offline handwriting recognition and online handwriting recognition. If handwriting is scanned and then understood by the computer, it is called offline handwriting recognition. In case, handwriting is recognized while writing, it is called online handwriting recognition. Online handwriting recognition captures a character as a set of strokes that are represented by a sequence of coordinate points. This way of capturing characters becomes conspicuous when dealing with strongly distorted characters written in the cursive style. Also, in online handwriting recognition, it is very natural for the user to detect and correct misrecognized characters on the spot by verifying the recognition results as they appear. The user is encouraged to modify his writing style so as to improve recognition accuracy. Also, a machine can be trained to a particular user's style. Samples of his misrecognized characters are stored to aid subsequent recognition. Thus both writer adaptation and machine adaptation is possible. Moreover, editing, annotating, and other applications that use direct pointing and manipulation are well suited to online handwriting recognition.

The online handwriting recognition has great potential to improve user and computer communication. Due to variability in handwriting styles and distortions caused by the digitizing process, even the best handwritten character recognizer is unreliable. The online handwriting recognition technology is used for identification of characters and it is used with devices such as personal digital assistant, cross pad and tablet PCs where a stylus is used to handwrite on a screen, after which the computer converts the handwritten text into digital text. In order to use these input devices, accuracy achieved by the handwriting recognizer must be sufficiently high so that it is acceptable by the user.

1.1.1 Handwriting styles variations

Handwriting styles variations depend on alignments and the different form of characters. These variations are geometrical in nature. Common geometrical properties are position, size, aspect ratio of strokes or characters, retraces, slant of strokes and number of strokes in a character. Fig. 1.1 and Fig. 1.2 describe some of the different styles that can be used to handwrite some of the characters of Gurmukhi script. Fig. 1.1 illustrates the few samples of Gurmukhi characters from five different writers. One can note that variations exist in each sample of a character. Fig. 1.2 illustrates five samples of few characters of Gurmukhi script from individual writers. One can note that some kind of variations also exists in each sample of a character although such samples share high degree of similarities. The shape of a character is also influenced by the word in which it is appearing. Characters can look similar although their number of strokes, and the drawing order and direction of the strokes may vary considerably. The writing samples in this book are of Indic script Gurmukhi.

Fig. 1.1: Variation in some of the Gurmukhi characters by five writers.

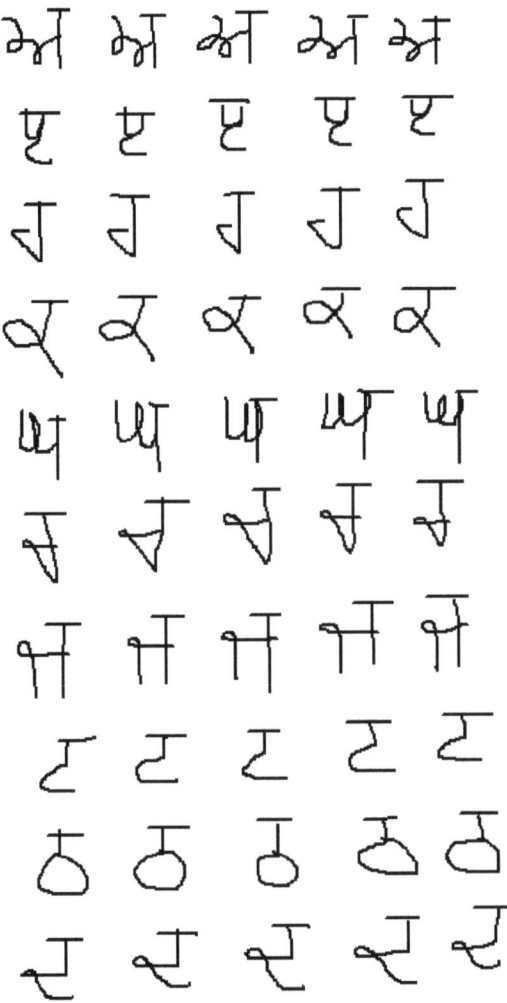

Fig. 1.2: Variation in some of the Gurmukhi characters handwritten by same writer.

1.1.2 Constrained and unconstrained handwriting

Handwriting styles could be constrained or unconstrained. Constrained handwriting is boxed discrete and spaced discrete in nature. Unconstrained handwriting is cursive or mixed cursive in nature. In boxed discrete handwriting, each character is written inside a special box. Fig. 1.3 illustrates the boxed discrete handwriting. When each character is written separately with spaces and no character touches other character is called spaced discrete handwriting. If each character is written separately and touches other characters, it is referred as run-on discrete handwriting. When characters in one word are connected and strokes are used more than once in individual character, it is referred to cursive handwriting. It is observed that most of the people write in mixed cursive styles that includes mixture of spaced, run-on discrete and cursive styles handwriting. Spaced discrete, run-on discrete, cursive and mixed cursive handwriting styles are illustrated in Fig. 1.4. It is a difficult task to recognize cursive handwriting due to great amount of variability. Each writer is having one's own speed of writing and uses different shapes to represent characters. Also, in cursive handwriting no clear boundaries are specified between characters to distinguish between them.

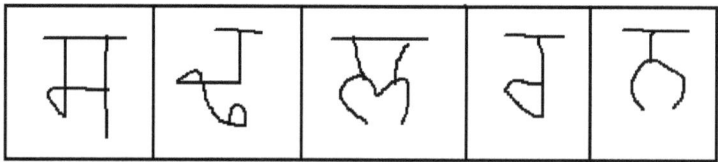

Fig. 1.3: Boxed discrete handwriting.

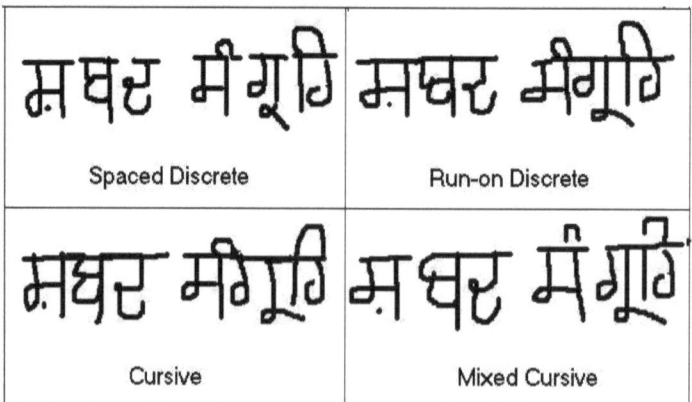

Fig. 1.4: Different styles of writing 'Sbd sMg@ih' in Gurmukhi.

1.1.3 Personal, situational and material factors

The personal factors in handwriting variations include writers' handedness. A writer is either left handed or right handed. It has been noted that left and right handed people use different positions and directions in handwriting. A good recognition requires neat and clean handwriting. In most of the cases, it has been noted that neat and clean handwriting do not take place as handwriting of people also depends on their profession.

The situational factors depend on the way of presentation of writing. The way of presentation could be stressful or in haste or distraction while writing. The material factors depend on the hardware used in writing. The material used in writing may provide comfort or discomfort to writer that result into variations in handwriting. This includes the position and size of writing board. The length of the writing line or the size of the writing boxes for characters could have effect on the handwriting style.

1.1.4 Writer dependent vs. writer independent recognition systems

Writer dependent and writer independent are the two categories of handwriting recognition system. These categories depend on the data with which recognition systems have been trained. The system that is based on known writing styles is called writer dependent system. The writer dependent systems are expert in certain handwriting styles and include recognition constraints with respect to stored handwriting styles. Therefore, a writer dependent system is trained with data collected from the writers whose handwriting will be recognized in the future. Writer independent systems are meant for the unknown handwriting styles. Writer independent system is more difficult to develop in comparison with writer dependent system. It is because writer independent system needs to study all common aspects of handwriting. Also, writer independent system demands all possible options to store handwriting variations in the database. Writer dependent recognition systems have achieved better recognition accuracy in comparison to writer independent recognition systems. In practical situations, writer independent recognition systems are more in demand as it includes recognition of unknown handwriting.

In the mid-seventies, digitizer tablets were available in which resistive technique and analog to digital conversion technique were used. It was possible to measure the pen tip using these tablets. A number of technologies were available for tablets or writing pads. These technologies were based on electronic or electromagnetic or electrostatic or pressure sensitive techniques and the tablets with combination of input and output digitizer or display on same surface were most common in handwriting recognition.

The established procedure to recognize online handwritten characters includes following phases or components: data collection, preprocessing, feature extraction or computation of features, segmentation, recognition and post-processing. These phases with their flow are listed in Fig. 1.5. The sections 1.2 to 1.7 explain role of each component.

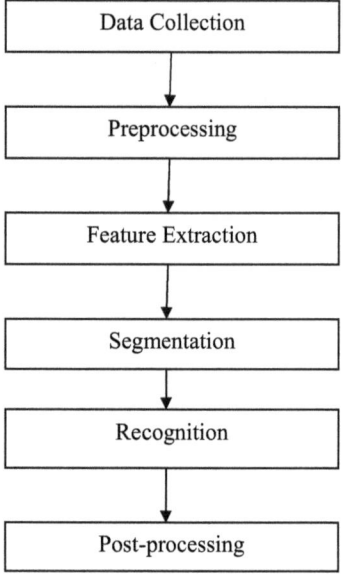

Fig. 1.5: Phases of online handwriting recognition.

1.2 Data collection

Online handwriting recognition requires a transducer that captures the writing as it is written. The most common of these devices is the electronic tablet or digitizer. These devices uses a pen that is digital in nature. Data collection is the first phase in online handwriting recognition that collects the sequence of coordinate points of the moving pen. A typical pen includes two actions, namely, PenDown and PenUp. The connected parts of the pen trace between PenDown and PenUp is called a stroke. These pen traces are sampled at constant rate, therefore these pen traces are evenly distributed in time and not in space. The common names of electronic tablet or digitizer are personal digital assistant, cross pad (or pen tablet) and tablet PC. The appearances of personal digital assistant, cross pad and tablet PC are shown in Fig. 1.6.

 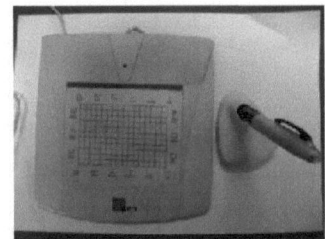 

Personal Digital Assistant   Cross pad or pen tablet   Tablet PC

Fig. 1.6: Commonly used hardware devices for capturing handwriting.

Common personal digital assistants available in the market are Amstrad, PenPad PDA 600, Apple, Newton Messagepad 2000, Casio, Z-7000, OmniGo 100, IBM, IBM WorkPad, Motorola, Marco, Envoy, Sharp, Zaurus ZR-5000FX, Zaurus ZR-5800FX, Sony, PIC-1000, Digital, SA-110 StrongARM, Tungsten, Nokia and HTC etc.

Cross pads available in the market are Badger, Cyrix, WebPAD, Fujitsu, 325Point, 325Point RF, Stylistic 500, Stylistic RF, IBM, iPen by UC-Logic, ThinkPad 730T, Kalidor, K2000, K2100, Microslate, Datellite 400L, Telepad, SL, Toshiba, Dynapad T200, T200CS, Tusk, SuperTABLET II, Zenith, CruisePAD 200, IBM, IBM 2488 Pen-Based Computer Model 300,MiniWriter & ScriptWriter XL by DES, Fujitsu (PoquetPad Plus RF) and Inforite (Phoenix, AS1050) etc.

Tablet PCs that are available in the market include Acer - TravelMate C110, Fujitsu – LifeBook 3000, Gateway – M275, IBM – Think Pad, Sharp – Actius 10W, Sotec – Afina AT380B, Toshiba – Portege M200, WinTop – XP Tablet PC, HP – Tablet PC TC1100, Amtek – iTablet 200 and Panasonic – ToughBook C-18 etc.

The selection of these hardware devices is mainly based on compatibility with operating system in use, active area dimensions and report rate of pen movements.

1.3 Preprocessing

Preprocessing phase in handwriting recognition is applied to remove noise or distortions present in input text due to hardware and software limitations *vis-à-vis* smooth handwriting. These noise or distortions include irregular size of text, missing points during pen movement collections, jitter present in text, left or right bend in handwriting and uneven distances of points from neighbouring positions. In online handwriting recognition, preprocessing includes five common steps, namely, size normailization and centering, interpolating missing points, smoothing, slant correction and resampling of points. These steps are illustrated in Fig. 1.7.

Size normalization depends on how user moves the pen on writing pad. Centering is required when pen is moved along the border of writing pad. High speed of handwriting results into missing points. These missing points can be interpolated using various techniques such as Bezier interpolation. Smoothing of input handwriting is required to remove jitter in handwriting. Smoothing usually averages a point with its neighbors. Slant correction and normalizing slant is required to correct the shape of input handwritten character as most of the writers handwriting is bend to left or right directions. Handwritten words are usually slanted or italicized due to the mechanism of handwriting and the personality. The main techniques for slant estimation and correction are run length based technique, projection method, extrema method and generalized chain code estimator. Resampling of points refers to the points in the list to be equidistant from neighbouring points as far as feasible. It means that new data points are calculated on the basis of the original points of list. The resampling techniques have been discussed in literature with respect to retain information about corner points.

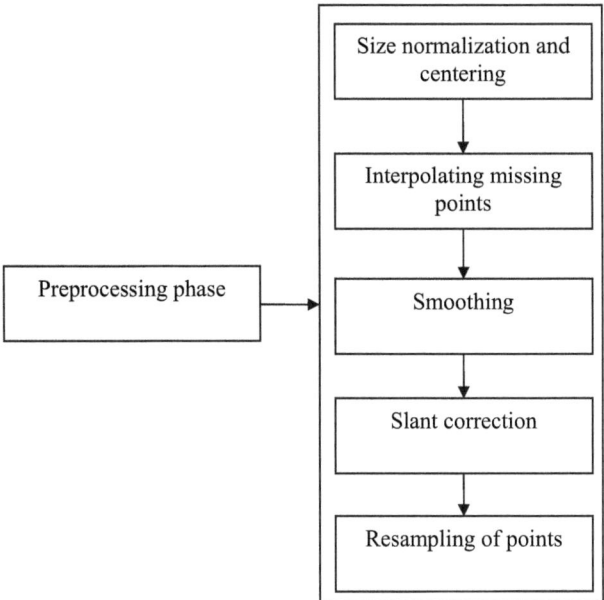

Fig. 1.7: Common steps in preprocessing phase.

1.4 Feature extraction or computation of features

Features are classified into two categories, namely, low-level and high-level features. A few neighbouring points estimate low-level features where as high-level features are estimated on larger scale than low-level features. High-level features in Gurmukhi script are those which provide useful information such as loops, crossings, headline, straight line and dots. These features are derived on the basis of calculating low-level features such as directions, positions, slope, area, slant *etc*. in a stroke.

In the process of handwriting recognition, it is important to identify correct features. Feature extraction is essential for efficient data representation and for further processing. Also, high recognition performance could be achieved by selecting suitable feature extraction method. Computational complexity of a classification problem can also be reduced if suitable features are selected. Features vary from one script to another script and the method that gives better result for a particular script cannot be applied for other scripts. Also, there is no standard method for computing features of a script. It is worth to note that features must vary to a reasonable extent and must be available in different users' cursive handwriting. Also, these features should be measurable through algorithms. These algorithms will improve the recognition accuracy.

1.5 Segmentation

Segmentation is one of the phases of handwriting recognition in which data are represented at character or stroke level so that nature of each character or stroke can be studied individually. Segmentation is classified into two categories: external segmentation and internal segmentation. External segmentation is performed prior to recognition. Segmentation performed during the process of recognition is called internal segmentation. External segmentation provides greater interactivity, savings of computation, and simplifies the job of the recognizer It has been noted that segmentation study in offline handwriting recognition system is beneficial to understand segmentation in online handwriting recognition system as word level segmentation is one of the common task in offline and online handwriting recognition systems. Both offline and online handwriting recognition systems identify characters or strokes in word level segmentation. Next paragraph reviews the literature of segmentation in offline handwriting recognition systems.

1.6 Recognition

Statistical, syntactical and structural, neural network and elastic matching are the common handwriting recognition methods

1.6.1 Statistical methods

In statistical approach, each pattern is represented in terms of d features and is viewed as a point in d dimensional space. This involves selection of features that all pattern vectors belonging to different categories or classes to occupy disjoint region in a d dimensional space. The statistical methods are based on prior probabilities of classes and assume variations in natural handwriting as stochastic in nature. Statistical methods are classified as parametric and non-parametric methods. In parametric methods, handwriting samples are statistical variables from distribution that is characterized by a set of parameters and each class includes its own distribution parameters. The selection of parameters is based on training data. Hidden Markov Model (HMM) is the common example of parametric methods. Non-parametric methods are directly estimated from training data. The k-nearest neighbors are the common non-parametric methods. Parametric methods are preferred as compared to non-parametric methods as parametric methods are computationally easier than non-parametric methods. HMM is the most widely used parametric statistical method applied to online handwriting recognition systems. HMM is in use for almost four decades from now. Initially, HMMs were applied to speech recognition.

1.6.2 Structural and syntactical methods

Structural and syntactical methods are related to handwritten patterns where structures and grammar are considered. Structural recognition provides a description of how the given pattern is constructed from the primitives. This paradigm has been used in situations where the patterns have a definite structure which can be captured in terms of a set of rules, such as waveforms, textured images, and shape analysis of contours. In syntactic pattern recognition, a formal analogy is drawn between the structure of patterns and the syntax of a language. The patterns are viewed as sentences belonging to a language, primitives are viewed as the alphabet of the language, and the sentences are generated according to a grammar. Thus, a large collection of complex patterns can be described by a small number of primitives and grammatical rules. The grammar for each pattern class must be inferred from the available training samples. The chain codes are widely used structural representations of online handwriting. Chain code means that a stroke is temporarily divided into segments and segments are coded. These segments are small straight lines of equal lengths and consider information as directions, angles, geometric information in segments.

1.6.3 Neural network methods

Neural networks can be viewed as parallel computing systems consisting of an extremely large number of simple processors with many interconnections. Neural network models attempt to use some organizational principles such as learning, generalization, adaptability, fault tolerance, distributed representation and computation in a network of weighted directed graphs in which the nodes are artificial neurons and directed edges are connections between neuron outputs and neuron inputs. The main characteristics of neural networks are that they have the ability to learn complex nonlinear input-output relationships, use sequential training procedures and adapt themselves to the data. The most commonly used neural networks for pattern classification tasks are feed-forward network, which include multilayer perceptron and radial basis function networks. These networks are organized into layers and have unidirectional connections between the layers. Another popular network is the self-organizing map or kohonen network.

1.6.4 Elastic matching methods

Elastic matching is a generic operation in pattern recognition which is used to determine the similarity between two entities. The pattern to be recognized is matched against the stored template while taking into account all allowable changes. The similarity measure can be optimized based on available training set. Elastic matching is computationally demanding but with availability of faster processors, this approach is feasible. Elastic matching is often called deformable template, flexible matching, or nonlinear template matching. Elastic matching works very well for writer dependent data and does not require a relatively large amount of training data In early works, Fujimoto used elastic matching for recognition of scanned images. In this system a handwritten FORTRAN program is digitized and converted to ASCII code. After digitization, the patterns are thinned and then they are coded into directions in order to build sequence of points.

1.7   Post-processing

Post-processing refers to the procedure of correcting misclassified results by applying linguistic knowledge. All the possible outcomes of an individual character are studied in terms of graph and the best suitable nature of character is depicted. Post-processing is processing of the output from shape recognition. Language information can increase the accuracy obtained by pure shape recognition. For handwriting input, some shape recognizers yield a single string of characters, while others yield a number of alternatives for each character, often with a measure of confidence for each alternative. A postprocessor can operate on this information to obtain estimates for larger linguistic units, such as words. When the shape recognizer yields a single choice for each character, string correction algorithms are applicable. Alternate choices provide more information for post-processing. In post-processing, a dictionary can be used to restrict the character combinations. This can be implemented as a grammar that specifies all possible combinations of characters.

CHAPTER 2

USER INTERFACE DEVELOPMENT

2.1 DATA COLLECTION PHASE

A typical format of online handwriting data is a sequence of coordinate points of the moving pen point. Connected parts of the pen trace, in which the pen point is touching the writing surface, are called strokes. The pen trace is usually sampled with a constant rate and thus data points are evenly distributed in time but not in space. When the speed of writing is slow, the sample points are located densely on the true pen trace, whereas quick writing produces sparsely located points. One can note that the speed of writing typically slows down on sharp corners, in the beginning of the stroke and at the end of stroke. It also slows down if writer is feeling hesitation in writing or taking a pause. Sampling rate and resolution should be so high that the sampled data points represent the true pen trace correctly. Naturally, the selection of suitable level of sampling rate and resolution depends on the writing speed and the scale of the meaningful pen trace features. If sampling rate is too low, odd corners will be introduced on the sampled pen trace and some of the real corners and miniscule trace features can be missed.

Pen movements are generated from pen and tablet being used in the handwriting process. These pen movements are stored in a list having each node as a recorded point. A point represents x and y coordinates of view port. In Gurmukhi, each character is a group of one or more strokes as illustrated in Fig. 2.1 for character '**K**'. A stroke is a list that includes recorded points stored in sequential order such that lines joining these points represent the stroke as a curve as shown in Fig. 2.2. Start and end of a stroke depend on PenDown and PenUp function of the input device in use. PenMove function is followed by PenDown function and ends up with PenUp function.

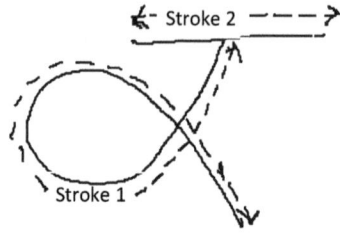

Fig. 2.1: Character '**K**' written with two strokes.

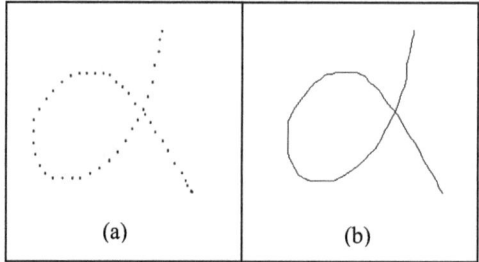

Fig. 2.2(a): Points collected while writing a stroke.
Fig. 2.2(b): Shape of stroke after joining these consecutive points.

We have developed an online handwritten Gurmukhi character recognizer which provides a graphical user interface to display the collected data from pen movements. This application collects input pen movements and further stores these pen movements in a list and also in a text file. Text file storage is required to retain original pen movements that are required at later stages whereas list storage is sent for preprocessing: the next stage of recognition process. Also, text file storage helps in verifying the input stroke shape with the help of graphical software such as, MS-Excel. Fig. 2.3 shows the graphical user interface of developed application and Fig. 2.4 depicts the screen shot of the data stored in text file. Fig. 2.5 shows the shape of collected stroke in MS-Excel.

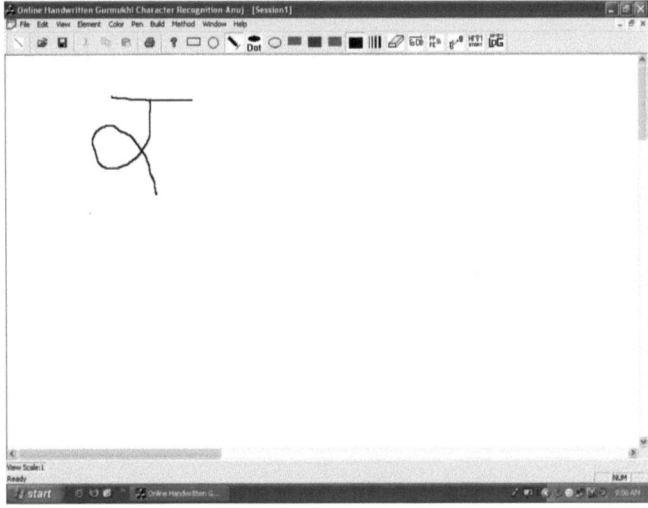

Fig. 2.3: Graphical user interface of developed application displaying input handwritten character.

Fig. 2.4: Screen shot of text file containing collected data of handwritten character in Fig. 2.3.

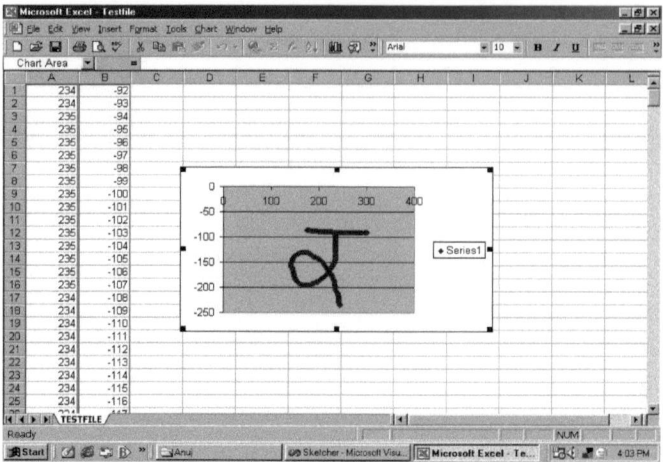

Fig. 2.5: Input handwritten character in MS-Excel as drawn in Fig. 2.3.

2.2 Interface development Class File

```cpp
// HWRAnujView.cpp : implementation of the CHWRAnujView class
//

#include "stdafx.h"

#include "ChildFrm.h"
#include "ScaleDialog.h"
#include "TextDialog.h"
#include "ToolsDialog.h"
#include "InputWordDialog.h"
#include "OurConstants.h"
#include "DataFile.h"
#include "Math.h"
#include "HWRAnuj.h"
#include "String.h"
#include "Stdlib.h"
#include "Elements.h"
#include "Preprocessing.h"
#include "GraphDialog.h"
#include "Graph.h"
#include "HWRAnujDoc.h"
#include "HWRAnujView.h"


#ifdef _DEBUG
#define new DEBUG_NEW
#undef THIS_FILE
static char THIS_FILE[] = __FILE__;
#endif

// CHWRAnujView

IMPLEMENT_DYNCREATE(CHWRAnujView, CScrollView)

BEGIN_MESSAGE_MAP(CHWRAnujView, CScrollView)
    //{{AFX_MSG_MAP(CHWRAnujView)
    ON_WM_LBUTTONDOWN()
    ON_WM_LBUTTONUP()
    ON_WM_MOUSEMOVE()
    ON_WM_CANCELMODE()
    ON_COMMAND(ID_MOVE, OnMove)
    ON_COMMAND(ID_DELETE, OnDelete)
    ON_WM_RBUTTONUP()
    ON_WM_RBUTTONDOWN()
    ON_COMMAND(ID_SENDTOBACK, OnSendtoback)
    ON_COMMAND(ID_VIEW_SCALE, OnViewScale)
    ON_COMMAND(ID_ADD_FILE, OnAddFile)
    ON_COMMAND(ID_ADD_FILE_CONFIRM, OnAddFileConfirm)
    ON_COMMAND(ID_COLLECT_CANCEL, OnCollectCancel)
    ON_COMMAND(ID_INPUT_WORD, OnInputWord)
    ON_COMMAND(ID_Preprocessing, OnPreprocessing)
    //}}AFX_MSG_MAP
    // Standard printing commands
    ON_COMMAND(ID_FILE_PRINT, CView::OnFilePrint)
    ON_COMMAND(ID_FILE_PRINT_DIRECT, CView::OnFilePrint)
```

```
        ON_COMMAND(ID_FILE_PRINT_PREVIEW, CView::OnFilePrintPreview)
END_MESSAGE_MAP()

// CHWRAnujView construction/destruction

CHWRAnujView::CHWRAnujView()
{
    // TODO: add construction code here

    m_FirstPoint=CPoint(0,0);
    m_SecondPoint=CPoint(0,0);
    m_pTempElement=NULL;
    m_pSelected = NULL;

    m_MoveMode=FALSE;
    m_CursorPos=CPoint(0,0);
    m_FirstPos=CPoint(0,0);

    m_Scale=1; m_I=0, m_CharID=0; m_CEdit_Line=0;
    SetScrollSizes(MM_TEXT, CSize(0,0));
}

CHWRAnujView::~CHWRAnujView()
{
    m_PointListXY.RemoveAll();
}

BOOL CHWRAnujView::PreCreateWindow(CREATESTRUCT& cs)
{
    return CView::PreCreateWindow(cs);
}

// CHWRAnujView drawing

void CHWRAnujView::OnDraw(CDC* pDC)
{
    CHWRAnujDoc* pDoc = GetDocument();
    ASSERT_VALID(pDoc);

    POSITION aPos = pDoc->GetListHeadPosition();
    CElement* pElement=0;
    while(aPos)
    {
        pElement = pDoc->GetNext(aPos);
        if(pDC->RectVisible(pElement->GetBoundRect()))
            pElement->Draw(pDC,m_pSelected);
    }
}

// CHWRAnujView printing

BOOL CHWRAnujView::OnPreparePrinting(CPrintInfo* pInfo)
```

```
{
    // default preparation
    return DoPreparePrinting(pInfo);
}

void CHWRAnujView::OnBeginPrinting(CDC* /*pDC*/, CPrintInfo*
/*pInfo*/)
{
    // TODO: add extra initialization before printing
}

void CHWRAnujView::OnEndPrinting(CDC* /*pDC*/, CPrintInfo*
/*pInfo*/)
{
    // TODO: add cleanup after printing
}


// CHWRAnujView diagnostics

#ifdef _DEBUG
void CHWRAnujView::AssertValid() const
{
    CView::AssertValid();
}

void CHWRAnujView::Dump(CDumpContext& dc) const
{
    CView::Dump(dc);
}

CHWRAnujDoc* CHWRAnujView::GetDocument() // non-debug version is
inline
{
    ASSERT(m_pDocument->IsKindOf(RUNTIME_CLASS(CHWRAnujDoc)));
    return (CHWRAnujDoc*)m_pDocument;
}
#endif //_DEBUG


void CHWRAnujView::OnLButtonDown(UINT nFlags, CPoint point)
{

    CView::OnLButtonDown(nFlags, point);

    CClientDC aDC(this);
    OnPrepareDC(&aDC);
    aDC.DPtoLP(&point);

    if(m_MoveMode)
    {
        m_MoveMode=FALSE;
        m_pSelected=0;
        GetDocument()->UpdateAllViews(0);
        GetDocument()->SetModifiedFlag();
    }
    else
```

```cpp
    {
        CHWRAnujDoc* pDoc = GetDocument();
        if(pDoc->GetElementType() == TEXT)
        {
            CTextDialog aDlg;
            if(aDlg.DoModal() == IDOK)
            {
                CSize TextExtent = aDC.GetTextExtent(aDlg.m_TextString);
                CPoint BottomRt(point.x+TextExtent.cx,
                        point.y-TextExtent.cy);
                CText* pTextElement = new CText(point,
BottomRt,aDlg.m_TextString, pDoc->GetElementColor(),pDoc-
>GetPenStyle(), pDoc->GetPenWidth());
                pDoc->AddElement(pTextElement);
                pDoc->UpdateAllViews(0,0,pTextElement);
            }
            return;
        }
        if(pDoc->GetElementType() == CURVE)
        {
            m_PointListXY.AddTail(point);
        }
        m_FirstPoint=point;
        SetCapture();
    }


}

void CHWRAnujView::OnLButtonUp(UINT nFlags, CPoint point)
{

    CView::OnLButtonUp(nFlags, point);

    if(this == GetCapture())
        ReleaseCapture();

    if(m_pTempElement)
    {
        if(m_pTempElement->IsKindOf(RUNTIME_CLASS(CCurve)))
        {
            point.y = 1;    ///In English data storage it reprsents new stroke
            m_PointListXY.AddTail(point);
        }
        GetDocument()->AddElement(m_pTempElement);
        GetDocument()->UpdateAllViews(0,0,m_pTempElement);
        m_pTempElement=0;
    }

}

void CHWRAnujView::OnMouseMove(UINT nFlags, CPoint point)
{

    CView::OnMouseMove(nFlags,point);
```

```cpp
      CClientDC aDC(this);
      OnPrepareDC(&aDC);

      if(m_MoveMode)
      {
            aDC.DPtoLP(&point);
            MoveElement(aDC, point);
            return;
      }

      aDC.SetROP2(R2_NOTXORPEN);
      if(nFlags & MK_LBUTTON)
      {
            aDC.DPtoLP(&point);
            m_SecondPoint=point;
            if(m_pTempElement)
            {
                  if(CURVE==GetDocument()->GetElementType())
                  {
                        (static_cast<CCurve*>(m_pTempElement))-
>AddSegment(m_SecondPoint);

                        m_PointListXY.AddTail(point);
                        m_pTempElement->Draw(&aDC);
                        return;
                  }
                  m_pTempElement->Draw(&aDC);
                  delete m_pTempElement;
                  m_pTempElement=0;
            }
            m_pTempElement=CreateElement();
            m_pTempElement->Draw(&aDC);
      }
      else
      {
            CRect aRect;
            CElement* pCurrentElement = SelectElement(point);

            if(pCurrentElement != m_pSelected)
            {
                  if(m_pSelected)
                  {
                        aRect = m_pSelected->GetBoundRect();
                        aDC.LPtoDP(aRect);
                        aRect.NormalizeRect();
                        InvalidateRect(aRect,FALSE);
                  }
                  m_pSelected = pCurrentElement;
                  if(m_pSelected)
                  {
                        aRect = m_pSelected->GetBoundRect();
                        aDC.LPtoDP(aRect);
                        aRect.NormalizeRect();
                        InvalidateRect(aRect, FALSE);
                  }
            }
```

```
            }

    }

    void CHWRAnujView::MoveElement(CClientDC& aDC, const CPoint&
    point)
    {
            CSize Distance = point - m_CursorPos;
            m_CursorPos=point;
            if(m_pSelected)
            {
                    if(m_pSelected->IsKindOf(RUNTIME_CLASS(CText)))
                    {
                            CRect OldRect=m_pSelected->GetBoundRect();
                            m_pSelected->Move(Distance);
                            CRect NewRect=m_pSelected->GetBoundRect();
                            OldRect.UnionRect(&OldRect, &NewRect);
                            aDC.LPtoDP(OldRect);
                            OldRect.NormalizeRect();
                            InvalidateRect(&OldRect);
                            UpdateWindow();
                            m_pSelected->Draw(&aDC, m_pSelected);

                            return;
                    }

                    aDC.SetROP2(R2_NOTXORPEN);
                    m_pSelected->Draw(&aDC, m_pSelected);
                    m_pSelected->Move(Distance);
                    m_pSelected->Draw(&aDC, m_pSelected);
            }
    }

    CElement* CHWRAnujView :: CreateElement()
    {
            CHWRAnujDoc* pDoc=GetDocument();
            ASSERT_VALID(pDoc);

            switch(pDoc->GetElementType())
            {
            case RECTANGLE:
                    return new CRectangle(m_FirstPoint, m_SecondPoint,
                            pDoc->GetElementColor(),pDoc->GetPenStyle(),
                            pDoc->GetPenWidth());

            case CIRCLE:
                    return new CCircle(m_FirstPoint, m_SecondPoint,
                            pDoc->GetElementColor(),pDoc->GetPenStyle(),
                            pDoc->GetPenWidth());

            case CURVE:
                    return new CCurve(m_FirstPoint, m_SecondPoint,
                            pDoc->GetElementColor(), pDoc->GetPenStyle(),
                            pDoc->GetPenWidth());

            case LINE:
                    return new CLine(m_FirstPoint, m_SecondPoint,
```

```
                    pDoc->GetElementColor(),pDoc->GetPenStyle(),
                    pDoc->GetPenWidth());

        case ELLIPSE:
            return new CEllipse(m_FirstPoint, m_SecondPoint,
                    pDoc->GetElementColor(),pDoc->GetPenStyle(),
                    pDoc->GetPenWidth());

        default:
            AfxMessageBox("Bad Element Code", MB_OK);
            AfxAbort();
            return NULL;

    }
}

void CHWRAnujView::OnCancelMode()
{
    CView::OnCancelMode();

    // TODO: Add your message handler code here

}

void CHWRAnujView::OnUpdate(CView* pSender, LPARAM lHint,
CObject* pHint)
{
    // TODO: Add your specialized code here and/or call the base
class

    if(pHint)
    {
        CClientDC aDC(this);
        OnPrepareDC(&aDC);
        CRect aRect = static_cast<CElement*>(pHint)-
>GetBoundRect();
        aDC.LPtoDP(aRect);
        aRect.NormalizeRect();
        InvalidateRect(aRect);
    }
    else
        InvalidateRect(0);

}

void CHWRAnujView::OnInitialUpdate()
{
    ResetScrollSizes();
    CScrollView::OnInitialUpdate();

}

void CHWRAnujView::OnMove()
{
    // TODO: Add your command handler code here
    CClientDC aDC(this);
    OnPrepareDC(&aDC);
```

```cpp
        GetCursorPos(&m_CursorPos);
        ScreenToClient(&m_CursorPos);
        aDC.DPtoLP(&m_CursorPos);
        m_FirstPos=m_CursorPos;
        m_MoveMode=TRUE;
}

void CHWRAnujView::OnDelete()
{

        // TODO: Add your command handler code here
        CHWRAnujDoc* pDoc = GetDocument();
        if(m_pSelected)
        {
        //      CHWRAnujDoc* pDoc = GetDocument();
                pDoc->DeleteElement(m_pSelected);
                pDoc->UpdateAllViews(0);
                m_pSelected=0;
        }
        else
        {
                pDoc->DeleteAllElements();
                pDoc->UpdateAllViews(0);
                m_pSelected=0;
                m_Character.Empty();
        }
}

void CHWRAnujView::OnRButtonUp(UINT nFlags, CPoint point)
{
        CScrollView::OnRButtonUp(nFlags, point);

        //m_pSelected = SelectElement(point);

        CMenu aMenu;
        aMenu.LoadMenu(IDR_CURSOR_MENU);
        ClientToScreen(&point);

        if(m_pSelected)
                aMenu.GetSubMenu(0)-
>TrackPopupMenu(TPM_LEFTALIGN|TPM_RIGHTBUTTON,
                point.x, point.y, this);
        else
        {
                COLORREF Color = GetDocument()->GetElementColor();
                aMenu.CheckMenuItem(ID_COLOR_BLACK,

    (BLACK==Color?MF_CHECKED:MF_UNCHECKED)|MF_BYCOMMAND);
                aMenu.CheckMenuItem(ID_COLOR_RED,

    (RED==Color?MF_CHECKED:MF_UNCHECKED)|MF_BYCOMMAND);
                aMenu.CheckMenuItem(ID_COLOR_GREEN,

    (GREEN==Color?MF_CHECKED:MF_UNCHECKED)|MF_BYCOMMAND);
                aMenu.CheckMenuItem(ID_COLOR_BLUE,

    (BLUE==Color?MF_CHECKED:MF_UNCHECKED)|MF_BYCOMMAND);
```

```cpp
            WORD ElementType = GetDocument()->GetElementType();
            aMenu.CheckMenuItem(ID_ELEMENT_LINE,
        (LINE==ElementType?MF_CHECKED:MF_UNCHECKED)|MF_BYCOMMAND);
            aMenu.CheckMenuItem(ID_ELEMENT_RECTANGLE,
        (RECTANGLE==ElementType?MF_CHECKED:MF_UNCHECKED)|MF_BYCOMMAND);
            aMenu.CheckMenuItem(ID_ELEMENT_CIRCLE,
        (CIRCLE==ElementType?MF_CHECKED:MF_UNCHECKED)|MF_BYCOMMAND);
            aMenu.CheckMenuItem(ID_ELEMENT_ELLIPSE,
        (ELLIPSE==ElementType?MF_CHECKED:MF_UNCHECKED)|MF_BYCOMMAND);
            aMenu.CheckMenuItem(ID_ELEMENT_CURVE,
        (CURVE==ElementType?MF_CHECKED:MF_UNCHECKED)|MF_BYCOMMAND);
            aMenu.CheckMenuItem(ID_ELEMENT_TEXT,
        (TEXT==ElementType?MF_CHECKED:MF_UNCHECKED)|MF_BYCOMMAND);

            aMenu.GetSubMenu(1)->TrackPopupMenu(TPM_LEFTALIGN|TPM_RIGHTBUTTON,
            point.x, point.y, this);
      }
}

CElement* CHWRAnujView:: SelectElement(CPoint aPoint)
{
      CClientDC aDC(this);
      OnPrepareDC(&aDC);
      aDC.DPtoLP(&aPoint);

      CHWRAnujDoc* pDoc=GetDocument();
      CElement* pElement = 0;
      CRect aRect(0,0,0,0);
      POSITION aPos=pDoc->GetListTailPosition();

      while(aPos)
      {
            pElement = pDoc->GetPrev(aPos);
            aRect = pElement->GetBoundRect();
            if(aRect.PtInRect(aPoint))
                  return pElement;
      }
      return 0;
}

void CHWRAnujView::OnRButtonDown(UINT nFlags, CPoint point)
{

      CScrollView::OnRButtonDown(nFlags, point);
```

```cpp
        if(m_MoveMode)
        {
            CClientDC aDC(this);
            OnPrepareDC(&aDC);
            MoveElement(aDC, m_FirstPos);
            m_MoveMode=FALSE;
            m_pSelected=0;
            GetDocument()->UpdateAllViews(0);
            return;
        }
}

void CHWRAnujView::OnSendtoback()
{
    // TODO: Add your command handler code here
    GetDocument()->SendToBack(m_pSelected);
}

void CHWRAnujView::OnViewScale()
{
    // TODO: Add your command handler code here
    CScaleDialog aDlg;
    aDlg.m_Scale = m_Scale;
    if(aDlg.DoModal()==IDOK)
    {
        m_Scale = 1 + aDlg.m_Scale;

        CChildFrame* viewFrame=static_cast<CChildFrame*>(GetParentFrame());
        CString StatusMsg("View Scale:");
        StatusMsg += static_cast<char>('0'+m_Scale);
        viewFrame->m_StatusBar.GetStatusBarCtrl().SetText(StatusMsg,0,0);
        ResetScrollSizes();
        InvalidateRect(0);
    }
}

void CHWRAnujView::OnPrepareDC(CDC* pDC, CPrintInfo* pInfo)
{
    // TODO: Add your specialized code here and/or call the base class

    CScrollView::OnPrepareDC(pDC, pInfo);

    CHWRAnujDoc* pDoc = GetDocument();
    pDC->SetMapMode(MM_ANISOTROPIC);
    CSize DocSize = pDoc->GetDocSize();

    DocSize.cy = -DocSize.cy;
    pDC->SetWindowExt(DocSize);

    int xLogPixels = pDC->GetDeviceCaps(LOGPIXELSX);
    int yLogPixels = pDC->GetDeviceCaps(LOGPIXELSY);

    int xExtent = DocSize.cx * m_Scale + xLogPixels / 100;
    int yExtent = DocSize.cy * m_Scale + yLogPixels / 100;
```

```
            pDC->SetViewportExt(xExtent, -yExtent);
}

void CHWRAnujView ::ResetScrollSizes()
{
      CClientDC aDC(this);
      OnPrepareDC(&aDC);
      CSize DocSize = GetDocument()->GetDocSize();
      aDC.LPtoDP(&DocSize);
      SetScrollSizes(MM_TEXT, DocSize);
}

//Add To DB

void CHWRAnujView::OnCollectCancel()
{
      m_PointListXY.RemoveAll();
}
void CHWRAnujView::OnAddFileConfirm()
{


}

void CHWRAnujView::OnInputWord()
{
      CInputWordDialog *ObjIW;
      ObjIW = new CInputWordDialog;
      ObjIW->Create(IDD_INPUT_WORD);
      ObjIW->ShowWindow(1);

}

void CHWRAnujView::ListToArray()
{
      int i=0; CPoint Point;
      POSITION aPos = m_PointListXY.GetHeadPosition();
      m_PointArray.RemoveAll();
      if(aPos)
      {
            while(aPos)
            {
                  Point = m_PointListXY.GetNext(aPos);
                  m_PointArray.SetAtGrow(i++, Point);
            }
      }
}

CString CHWRAnujView::GetHandwrittenPoints()
{
      char b[20]; int i=0; CString strPoints; CPoint Point;
      strPoints = "S";
      while(i<m_PointArray.GetSize())
      {
            if(Point.y > 0) strPoints += "S";
            Point = m_PointArray.GetAt(i);
```

```
            strPoints += "X"; _gcvt_s(b,20,Point.x,9); strPoints
 += b;
            strPoints += "Y"; _gcvt_s(b,20,Point.y,9); strPoints
 += b;
            i++;
        }
        return strPoints;
}

void CHWRAnujView::OnAddFile()
{
    // TODO: Add your command handler code here
    if(m_PointListXY.GetSize()>0)
    {
        CPoint Point; CTime time; CString strTime,
SelectedWord, strPoints; CInputWordDialog ObjIW;
        time=time.GetCurrentTime(); strTime=time.Format("%d-
%B-%Y,%H-%M-%S,");
        ListToArray();
        SelectedWord = ObjIW.GetSelectedWord();
        strPoints = GetHandwrittenPoints();
        FileName = "CurrentWritersData.dat";
        if(!ObjF.Open(FileName, CStdioFile:: modeCreate |
CStdioFile::modeNoTruncate | CStdioFile::modeReadWrite))   ///to
create file or check if already exists
        {}
        Data = ",,,"; Data+=strTime; Data+=SelectedWord;
Data+=","; Data+=strPoints; Data+=";\n";
        ObjF.SeekToEnd(); ObjF.WriteString(Data);
        m_PointListXY.RemoveAll(); ObjF.Close();
    }
}

void CHWRAnujView::OnPreprocessing()
{
    int PPFlag;
    CGraphDialog ObjGD;
    if(m_PointListXY.GetSize()>0)
    {
        PPFlag = ObjPP.AddToPPList(&m_PointListXY);
        ObjGD.DoModal();
        m_PointListXY.RemoveAll();
    }
    else
        AfxMessageBox("Please input text to view Preprocessing
stages!!!");
}
```

```cpp
// HWRAnuj.cpp : Defines the class behaviors for the application.
//

#include "stdafx.h"
#include "HWRAnuj.h"

#include "MainFrm.h"
#include "ChildFrm.h"
#include "Elements.h"
#include "HWRAnujDoc.h"
#include "HWRAnujView.h"

#ifdef _DEBUG
#define new DEBUG_NEW
#undef THIS_FILE
static char THIS_FILE[] = __FILE__;
#endif


// CHWRAnujApp

BEGIN_MESSAGE_MAP(CHWRAnujApp, CWinApp)
    //{{AFX_MSG_MAP(CHWRAnujApp)
    ON_COMMAND(ID_APP_ABOUT, OnAppAbout)
    ON_COMMAND(ID_FILE_NEW, CWinApp::OnFileNew)
    ON_COMMAND(ID_FILE_OPEN, CWinApp::OnFileOpen)
    // Standard print setup command
    ON_COMMAND(ID_FILE_PRINT_SETUP, CWinApp::OnFilePrintSetup)
END_MESSAGE_MAP()


// CHWRAnujApp construction

CHWRAnujApp::CHWRAnujApp()
{
}


// The one and only CHWRAnujApp object

CHWRAnujApp theApp;


// CHWRAnujApp initialization

BOOL CHWRAnujApp::InitInstance()
{
    AfxEnableControlContainer();

    #ifdef _AFXDLL
    #else
    Enable3dControlsStatic();   // Call this when linking to MFC statically
    #endif

    SetRegistryKey(_T("Local AppWizard-Generated Applications"));
```

```cpp
        LoadStdProfileSettings();  // Load standard INI file options
(including MRU)

        CMultiDocTemplate* pDocTemplate;
        pDocTemplate = new CMultiDocTemplate(
            IDR_SKETCHTYPE,
            RUNTIME_CLASS(CHWRAnujDoc),
            RUNTIME_CLASS(CChildFrame),  // custom MDI child frame
            RUNTIME_CLASS(CHWRAnujView));
        AddDocTemplate(pDocTemplate);

        // create main MDI Frame window
        CMainFrame* pMainFrame = new CMainFrame;
        if (!pMainFrame->LoadFrame(IDR_MAINFRAME))
            return FALSE;
        m_pMainWnd = pMainFrame;

        // Enable drag/drop open
        m_pMainWnd->DragAcceptFiles();

        // Enable DDE Execute open
        EnableShellOpen();
        RegisterShellFileTypes(TRUE);

        // Parse command line for standard shell commands, DDE, file
open
        CCommandLineInfo cmdInfo;
        ParseCommandLine(cmdInfo);

        // Dispatch commands specified on the command line
        if (!ProcessShellCommand(cmdInfo))
            return FALSE;

        // The main window has been initialized, so show and update
it.
        m_nCmdShow = SW_MAXIMIZE;
        pMainFrame->ShowWindow(m_nCmdShow);
        pMainFrame->UpdateWindow();
        ///below line for show of unipen only/
        //CHWRAnujView obj; obj.OnRecognition();
        return TRUE;
}
```

```cpp
// CAboutDlg dialog used for App About

class CAboutDlg : public CDialog
{
public:
    CAboutDlg();

// Dialog Data
    //{{AFX_DATA(CAboutDlg)
    enum { IDD = IDD_ABOUTBOX };
    //}}AFX_DATA

    // ClassWizard generated virtual function overrides
    //{{AFX_VIRTUAL(CAboutDlg)
    protected:
    virtual void DoDataExchange(CDataExchange* pDX);    // DDX/DDV support
    //}}AFX_VIRTUAL

// Implementation
protected:
    //{{AFX_MSG(CAboutDlg)
        // No message handlers
    //}}AFX_MSG
    DECLARE_MESSAGE_MAP()
};

CAboutDlg::CAboutDlg() : CDialog(CAboutDlg::IDD)
{
    //{{AFX_DATA_INIT(CAboutDlg)
    //}}AFX_DATA_INIT
}

void CAboutDlg::DoDataExchange(CDataExchange* pDX)
{
    CDialog::DoDataExchange(pDX);
    //{{AFX_DATA_MAP(CAboutDlg)
    //}}AFX_DATA_MAP
}

BEGIN_MESSAGE_MAP(CAboutDlg, CDialog)
    //{{AFX_MSG_MAP(CAboutDlg)
        // No message handlers
    //}}AFX_MSG_MAP
END_MESSAGE_MAP()

// App command to run the dialog
void CHWRAnujApp::OnAppAbout()
{
    CAboutDlg aboutDlg;
    aboutDlg.DoModal();
}


// CHWRAnujApp message handlers
```

```cpp
// HWRAnujDoc.cpp : implementation of the CHWRAnujDoc class
1//


#include "stdafx.h"
#include "Elements.h"
#include "HWRAnuj.h"
#include "PenDialog.h"
#include "HWRAnujDoc.h"

#ifdef _DEBUG
#define new DEBUG_NEW
#undef THIS_FILE
static char THIS_FILE[] = __FILE__;
#endif


// CHWRAnujDoc

IMPLEMENT_DYNCREATE(CHWRAnujDoc, CDocument)

BEGIN_MESSAGE_MAP(CHWRAnujDoc, CDocument)
    //{{AFX_MSG_MAP(CHWRAnujDoc)
    ON_COMMAND(ID_COLOR_BLACK, OnColorBlack)
    ON_COMMAND(ID_COLOR_BLUE, OnColorBlue)
    ON_COMMAND(ID_COLOR_GREEN, OnColorGreen)
    ON_COMMAND(ID_COLOR_RED, OnColorRed)
    ON_COMMAND(ID_ELEMENT_CIRCLE, OnElementCircle)
    ON_COMMAND(ID_ELEMENT_CURVE, OnElementCurve)
    ON_COMMAND(ID_ELEMENT_LINE, OnElementLine)
    ON_COMMAND(ID_ELEMENT_RECTANGLE, OnElementRectangle)
    ON_UPDATE_COMMAND_UI(ID_COLOR_BLACK, OnUpdateColorBlack)
    ON_UPDATE_COMMAND_UI(ID_COLOR_BLUE, OnUpdateColorBlue)
    ON_UPDATE_COMMAND_UI(ID_COLOR_GREEN, OnUpdateColorGreen)
    ON_UPDATE_COMMAND_UI(ID_COLOR_RED, OnUpdateColorRed)
    ON_UPDATE_COMMAND_UI(ID_ELEMENT_CIRCLE, OnUpdateElementCircle)
    ON_UPDATE_COMMAND_UI(ID_ELEMENT_CURVE, OnUpdateElementCurve)
    ON_UPDATE_COMMAND_UI(ID_ELEMENT_LINE, OnUpdateElementLine)
    ON_UPDATE_COMMAND_UI(ID_ELEMENT_RECTANGLE, OnUpdateElementRectangle)
    ON_COMMAND(ID_ELEMENT_ELLIPSE, OnElementEllipse)
    ON_UPDATE_COMMAND_UI(ID_ELEMENT_ELLIPSE, OnUpdateElementEllipse)
    ON_COMMAND(ID_PEN_SOLID, OnPenSolid)
    ON_UPDATE_COMMAND_UI(ID_PEN_SOLID, OnUpdatePenSolid)
    ON_COMMAND(ID_PEN_DOT, OnPenDot)
    ON_UPDATE_COMMAND_UI(ID_PEN_DOT, OnUpdatePenDot)
    ON_COMMAND(ID_PEN_DASHED, OnPenDashed)
    ON_UPDATE_COMMAND_UI(ID_PEN_DASHED, OnUpdatePenDashed)
    ON_COMMAND(ID_PEN_DASHDOTDOT, OnPenDashdotdot)
    ON_UPDATE_COMMAND_UI(ID_PEN_DASHDOTDOT, OnUpdatePenDashdotdot)
    ON_COMMAND(ID_PEN_DASHDOT, OnPenDashdot)
    ON_UPDATE_COMMAND_UI(ID_PEN_DASHDOT, OnUpdatePenDashdot)
    ON_COMMAND(ID_PENWIDTH, OnPenwidth)
    ON_COMMAND(ID_ELEMENT_TEXT, OnElementText)
```

```cpp
        ON_UPDATE_COMMAND_UI(ID_ELEMENT_TEXT, OnUpdateElementText)
        //}}AFX_MSG_MAP
END_MESSAGE_MAP()


// CHWRAnujDoc construction/destruction

CHWRAnujDoc::CHWRAnujDoc()
{
        // TODO: add one-time construction code here
        m_Element = CURVE;
        m_Color = BLACK;
        m_PenStyle= SOLID;
        m_PenWidth=2;
        m_DocSize = CSize(3000,3000);
}

CHWRAnujDoc::~CHWRAnujDoc()
{

        POSITION aPosition = m_ElementList.GetHeadPosition();

        while(aPosition)
                delete m_ElementList.GetNext(aPosition);
        m_ElementList.RemoveAll();
}

BOOL CHWRAnujDoc::OnNewDocument()
{
        if (!CDocument::OnNewDocument())
                return FALSE;

        // TODO: add reinitialization code here
        // (SDI documents will reuse this document)

        return TRUE;
}



// CHWRAnujDoc serialization

void CHWRAnujDoc::Serialize(CArchive& ar)
{
        m_ElementList.Serialize(ar);
        if (ar.IsStoring())
        {
                // TODO: add storing code here
                ar<<m_Color<<m_Element<<m_PenWidth
                        <<m_DocSize<<m_PenWidth<<m_PenStyle;
        }
        else
        {
                // TODO: add loading code here
                ar>>m_Color>>m_Element>>m_PenWidth
                        >>m_DocSize>>m_PenWidth>>m_PenStyle;
```

```cpp
        }
}


// CHWRAnujDoc diagnostics

#ifdef _DEBUG
void CHWRAnujDoc::AssertValid() const
{
    CDocument::AssertValid();
}

void CHWRAnujDoc::Dump(CDumpContext& dc) const
{
    CDocument::Dump(dc);
}
#endif //_DEBUG


// CHWRAnujDoc commands

void CHWRAnujDoc::OnColorBlack()
{
    // TODO: Add your command handler code here
    m_Color = BLACK;
}

void CHWRAnujDoc::OnColorBlue()
{
    // TODO: Add your command handler code here
    m_Color = BLUE;
}

void CHWRAnujDoc::OnColorGreen()
{
    // TODO: Add your command handler code here
    m_Color = GREEN;
}

void CHWRAnujDoc::OnColorRed()
{
    // TODO: Add your command handler code here
    m_Color = RED;
}

void CHWRAnujDoc::OnElementCircle()
{
    // TODO: Add your command handler code here
    m_Element = CIRCLE;
}

void CHWRAnujDoc::OnElementCurve()
{
    // TODO: Add your command handler code here
    m_Element = CURVE;

}
```

```cpp
void CHWRAnujDoc::OnElementLine()
{
    // TODO: Add your command handler code here
    m_Element = LINE;
}

void CHWRAnujDoc::OnElementRectangle()
{
    // TODO: Add your command handler code here
    m_Element = RECTANGLE;
}

void CHWRAnujDoc::OnUpdateColorBlack(CCmdUI* pCmdUI)
{
    // TODO: Add your command update UI handler code here
    pCmdUI->SetCheck(m_Color==BLACK);
    if(m_Color==BLACK)
        pCmdUI->SetText("BLACK");
    else
        pCmdUI->SetText("black");
}

void CHWRAnujDoc::OnUpdateColorBlue(CCmdUI* pCmdUI)
{
    // TODO: Add your command update UI handler code here
    pCmdUI->SetCheck(m_Color==BLUE);
    if(m_Color==BLUE)
        pCmdUI->SetText("BLUE");
    else
        pCmdUI->SetText("blue");
}

void CHWRAnujDoc::OnUpdateColorGreen(CCmdUI* pCmdUI)
{
    // TODO: Add your command update UI handler code here
    pCmdUI->SetCheck(m_Color==GREEN);
    if(m_Color==GREEN)
        pCmdUI->SetText("GREEN");
    else
        pCmdUI->SetText("green");
}

void CHWRAnujDoc::OnUpdateColorRed(CCmdUI* pCmdUI)
{
    // TODO: Add your command update UI handler code here
    pCmdUI->SetCheck(m_Color==RED);
    if(m_Color==RED)
        pCmdUI->SetText("RED");
    else
        pCmdUI->SetText("red");
}

void CHWRAnujDoc::OnUpdateElementCircle(CCmdUI* pCmdUI)
{
    // TODO: Add your command update UI handler code here
    pCmdUI->SetCheck(m_Element==CIRCLE);
```

```cpp
}

void CHWRAnujDoc::OnUpdateElementCurve(CCmdUI* pCmdUI)
{
    // TODO: Add your command update UI handler code here
    pCmdUI->SetCheck(m_Element==CURVE);
}

void CHWRAnujDoc::OnUpdateElementLine(CCmdUI* pCmdUI)
{
    // TODO: Add your command update UI handler code here
    pCmdUI->SetCheck(m_Element==LINE);
}

void CHWRAnujDoc::OnUpdateElementRectangle(CCmdUI* pCmdUI)
{
    // TODO: Add your command update UI handler code here
    pCmdUI->SetCheck(m_Element==RECTANGLE);
}

void CHWRAnujDoc::OnElementEllipse()
{
    // TODO: Add your command handler code here
    m_Element = ELLIPSE;
}

void CHWRAnujDoc::OnUpdateElementEllipse(CCmdUI* pCmdUI)
{
    // TODO: Add your command update UI handler code here
    pCmdUI->SetCheck(m_Element==ELLIPSE);
}

void CHWRAnujDoc::OnPenSolid()
{
    // TODO: Add your command handler code here
    m_PenStyle = SOLID;
}

void CHWRAnujDoc::OnUpdatePenSolid(CCmdUI* pCmdUI)
{
    // TODO: Add your command update UI handler code here
    pCmdUI->SetCheck(m_PenStyle==SOLID);
}

void CHWRAnujDoc::OnPenDot()
{
    // TODO: Add your command handler code here
    m_PenStyle = DOT;
}

void CHWRAnujDoc::OnUpdatePenDot(CCmdUI* pCmdUI)
{
    // TODO: Add your command update UI handler code here
    pCmdUI->SetCheck(m_PenStyle==DOT);
}

void CHWRAnujDoc::OnPenDashed()
```

```cpp
{
    // TODO: Add your command handler code here
    m_PenStyle = DASH;
}

void CHWRAnujDoc::OnUpdatePenDashed(CCmdUI* pCmdUI)
{
    // TODO: Add your command update UI handler code here
    pCmdUI->SetCheck(m_PenStyle==DASH);
}

void CHWRAnujDoc::OnPenDashdotdot()
{
    // TODO: Add your command handler code here
    m_PenStyle = DASHDOTDOT;
}

void CHWRAnujDoc::OnUpdatePenDashdotdot(CCmdUI* pCmdUI)
{
    // TODO: Add your command update UI handler code here
    pCmdUI->SetCheck(m_PenStyle==DASHDOTDOT);
}

void CHWRAnujDoc::OnPenDashdot()
{
    // TODO: Add your command handler code here
    m_PenStyle = DASHDOT;
}

void CHWRAnujDoc::OnUpdatePenDashdot(CCmdUI* pCmdUI)
{
    // TODO: Add your command update UI handler code here
    pCmdUI->SetCheck(m_PenStyle==DASHDOT);
}

void CHWRAnujDoc::DeleteElement(CElement* pElement)
{
    if(pElement)
    {
        SetModifiedFlag();
        POSITION aPosition = m_ElementList.Find(pElement);
        m_ElementList.RemoveAt(aPosition);
        delete pElement;
    }
}

void CHWRAnujDoc::DeleteAllElements()
{
    POSITION aPosition = m_ElementList.GetHeadPosition();

    while(aPosition)
        delete m_ElementList.GetNext(aPosition);
    m_ElementList.RemoveAll();
}

void CHWRAnujDoc::SendToBack(CElement* pElement)
{
```

```
		if(pElement)
		{
			POSITION aPosition=m_ElementList.Find(pElement);
			m_ElementList.RemoveAt(aPosition);
			m_ElementList.AddHead(pElement);
		}
}

void CHWRAnujDoc::OnPenwidth()
{
	// TODO: Add your command handler code here
	CPenDialog aDlg;

	aDlg.m_PenWidth = m_PenWidth;
	if(aDlg.DoModal() == IDOK)
		m_PenWidth = aDlg.m_PenWidth;
}

void CHWRAnujDoc::OnElementText()
{
	// TODO: Add your command handler code here
	m_Element = TEXT;
}

void CHWRAnujDoc::OnUpdateElementText(CCmdUI* pCmdUI)
{
	// TODO: Add your command update UI handler code here
	pCmdUI->SetCheck(m_Element == TEXT);
}
```

CHAPTER 3

PREPROCESSING DEVELOPMENT

Preprocessing phase in online handwriting recognition is applied to remove noise present in input text due to hardware and software limitations *vis-a-vis* smooth handwriting. This noise exists in the input text in the form of sharp edges, non-centered text, uneven sizes of text and missing points in text trajectories due to high speed of handwriting and slants in characters. Preprocessing steps improve the overall recognition rate. It is one of the essential phases of online handwriting recognition and most of the researchers have discussed its challenges for various scripts from time to time.

We have performed five essential preprocessing steps in online handwritten Gurmukhi character recognition. These preprocessing steps are discussed in Subsections 3.1 to 3.5. Fig. 3.1 represents input handwritten stroke before preprocessing.

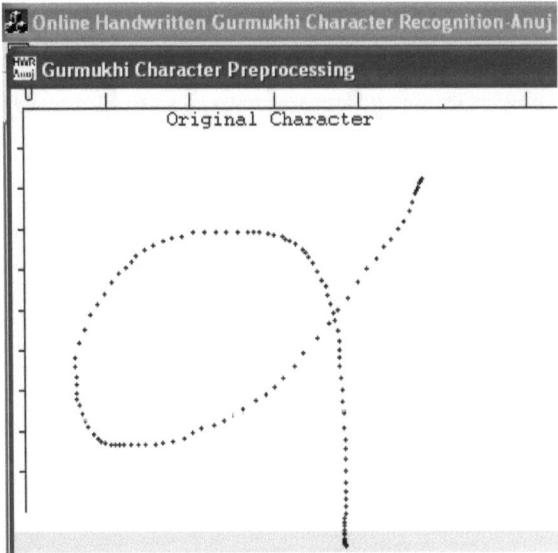

Fig. 3.1: Handwritten stroke before preprocessing.

As discussed in chapter 1, collected data is storage of pen movements in online handwriting recognition. These movements appear at various positions on viewport and joining these positions in first-cum-first-serve basis shows the appearance of drawn text. A character may consist of single or multiple strokes. The list formed in data collection includes nodes, where each node includes two fields, namely, point and stroke number. Here, the point represents x and y coordinates of view port and stroke number represents identity and sequential order of stroke. Also, stroke number helps in identifying similar points, gaps and crossings. If stroke 1 and stroke 2 include m_1 and m_2 points respectively, then the size 'n' of the list will be $m_1 + m_2$.

The pen movement consists of three functions, namely, PenDown, PenMove and PenUp. When one presses, moves, lifts the pen up consecutively, and more than one point collected, the stroke number is incremented. PenMove function stores movements of pen on writing pad. The points of the list are denoted by $P_i(x, y), i = 1, 2, \ldots, n;$ where n is total number of points in the list. For sake of brevity, we have used P_i for the point $P_i(x, y)$ in various algorithms in this Chapter and subsequent Chapters. Let us also denote the x-coordinate of $P_i(x, y)$ by P_{i_x} and its y-coordinate by P_{i_y}. PenUp indicates end of stroke and this process of storing the points is repeated till the last stroke. The data collected in this way is segmented at stroke level.

3.1 Size normalization and centering of stroke

Size of the input stroke depends on how user moves the pen on writing pad. Stroke is not generally centered when the pen is moved along the border of writing pad. Size normalization and centering of stroke is a necessary process that should be performed in order to recognize a character. This can be achieved by comparing input stroke border frame with assumed fixed size frame and further can be moved along with the assumed center location. The algorithm for size normalization and centering of stroke is given below:

In this algorithm, origin of the frame of reference is taken as (x_0, y_0) and the set of pixels in which a Gurmukhi character is drawn is given by $\{(x, y): 0 \leq x \leq l_x, l_y \leq y \leq 0\}$, where, l_x and l_y are the lengths in x and y directions. It may be noted that there are n pixels in a Gurmukhi character.

Algorithm 3.1

1. Set $L_x = 200$(pixels), $L_y = 200$(pixels).

2. $P_{i_x} = P_{i_x} \times \left(\frac{l_x}{L_x}\right), P_{i_y} = P_{i_y} \times \left(\frac{l_y}{L_y}\right)$ ∀ points P_i in list, $i = 1, 2, \ldots, n$.

3. $P_{i_x} = P_{i_x} \pm x_0, P_{i_y} = P_{i_y} \pm y_0$ ∀ points P_i in list, $i = 1, 2, \ldots, n$.

This algorithm normalizes the stroke in size and places it in the centre of fixed frame as depicted in Fig. 2.2. With this algorithm, we retain original aspect ratio of the character. Fig. 2.3 contains the character after size normalization and centering.

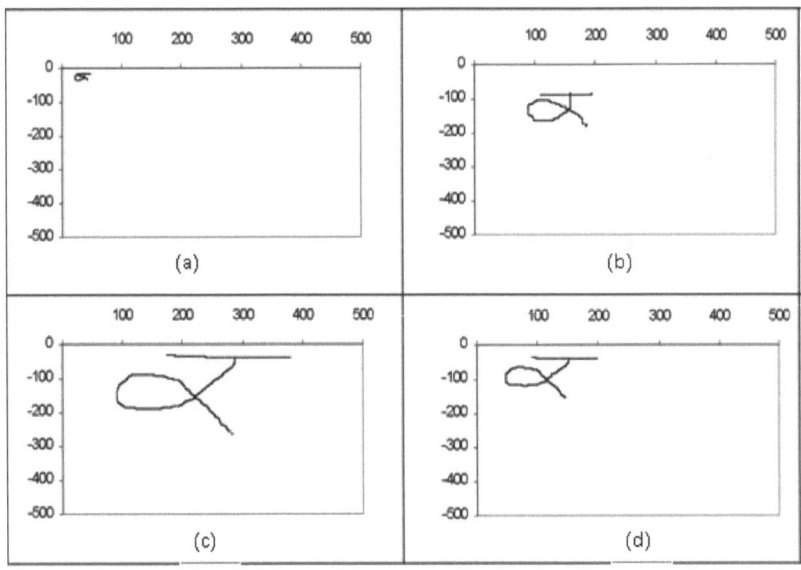

Fig. 2.2(a): Input character of size smaller than 200×200 pixels.

Fig. 2.2(b): Transformation of character (given in Fig. 2.7(a)) after size normalization and centering.

Fig. 2.2(c): Input character of size larger than 200×200 pixels.

Fig. 2.2(d): Transformation of character (given in Fig. 2.7(c)) after size normalization and centering.

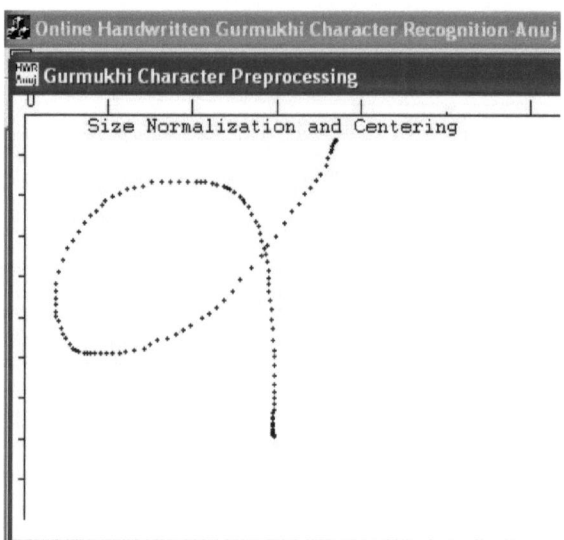

Fig. 2.3: Handwritten stroke after size normalization and centering.

3.2 Interpolating missing points

As mentioned in Section 2.1, the stroke drawn with high speed will have missing points. These missing points can be calculated using various techniques such as Bezier and B-Spline (Unser *et al.*, 1993). In pesent study, piecewise Bezier interpolation has been used because it helps to interpolate points among fixed number of points. This further helps in equidistancing of points, as discussed in Subsection 2.2.5. In piecewise interpolation technique, a set of consecutive four points is considered for obtaining the Bezier curve. The next set of four points gives the next Bezier curve. Algorithm used for interpolation of missing points by using Bezier curve is given below.

Algorithm 3.2

1. Create an empty list L for storing the points generated from the *Bezier* function.
2. Set t = number of strokes in the list and set $k = 1$.
3. Repeat step 4 for each stroke k, until $k \leq t$.
4.
    (a) Calculate m as the total number of points in the current stroke k.
    (b) If $(m \geq 4)$ then

    CALL *Bezier*$(P_i, P_{i+1}, P_{i+2}, P_{i+3})$ $\forall$ points P_i, $i = 1, 2, \ldots, m-3$

Else

>   Set $k = k + 1$.

End if

(c) Update list L by incorporating the new points as the consecutive points obtained through *Bezier* function.

(d) Set $k = k + 1$.

5. Exit.

function Bezier$(P_i, P_{i+1}, P_{i+2}, P_{i+3})$

1. u is a variable such that $0 \leq u \leq 1$.
2. Set $u = 0.2$ and $\Delta u = 0.2$.
3. Repeat steps 4 and 5 until $u \leq 1$.
4. Calculate x coordinate of new point as

$$P_{i_x} \times (1-u)^3 + P_{(i+1)_x} \times 3 \times u \times (1-u)^2 + P_{(i+2)_x} \times 3 \times u^2 \times (1-u) + P_{(i+3)_x} \times u^3,$$

and calculate y coordinate of new point as

$$P_{i_y} \times (1-u)^3 + P_{(i+1)_y} \times 3 \times u \times (1-u)^2 + P_{(i+2)_y} \times 3 \times u^2 \times (1-u) + P_{(i+3)_y} \times u^3.$$

5. Set $u = u + \Delta u$.
6. Return.

Fig. 3.4 contains the character after interpolating missing points.

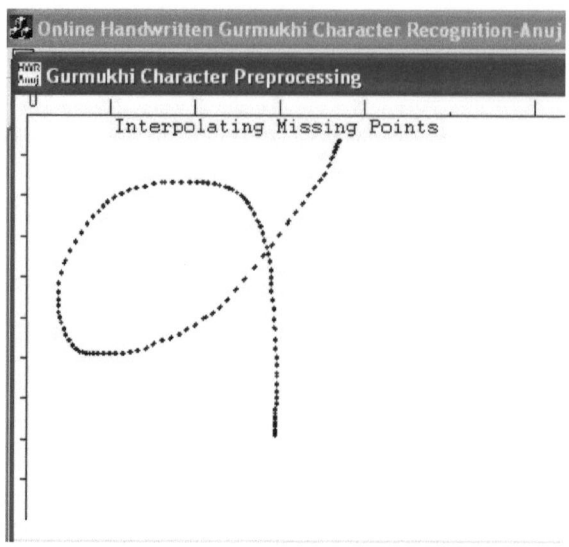

Fig. 3.4: Handwritten stroke after Interpolation of points.

3.3 Smoothing of stroke

Flickers exist in handwriting because of individual handwriting style and the hardware used. These flickers can be removed by modifying each point of the list with mean value of k-neighbors and the angle subtended at k^{th} position from each end (Kavallieratou *et al.*, 2002). Fig. 2.10 depicts how 2-neighbors from each side can be considered for this purpose. In this figure five points of the list, generated in the previous step, have been used for smoothing of the stroke. The point P_i has been modified with the help of points $P_{i-2}, P_{i-1}, P_{i+1}$ and P_{i+2}. It is worth mentioning here that if we consider three points then it will not affect the nature of stroke and if we consider more than five points then we tend to loose the nature of stroke in terms of sharp edges.

Algorithm 3.3 contains the steps that have been used for smoothing of a stroke.

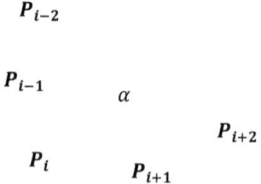

Fig. 3.5: Formation of angle α at point P_i.

Algorithm 3.3

1. Set t = number of strokes in the list and set $k = 1$.
2. Repeat step 3 for each stroke k, until $k \leq t$.
3.
    (a) Calculate m as the total number of points in the current stroke k.
    (b) Repeat steps (c) and (d) $\forall$ points P_i, $i = 3, 4, \ldots, m - 2$.
    (c) Calculate $\alpha = \angle P_{i-2} P_i P_{i+2}$.
    (d) Set $P_{i_x} = (P_{(i-2)_x} + P_{(i-1)_x} + \alpha \times P_{i_x} + P_{(i+1)_x} + P_{(i+2)_x})/(2 \times 2 + \alpha)$.
    Set $P_{i_y} = (P_{(i-2)_y} + P_{(i-1)_y} + \alpha \times P_{i_y} + P_{(i+1)_y} + P_{(i+2)_y})/(2 \times 2 + \alpha)$.
4. Set $k = k + 1$.
5. Exit.

3.4 Slant correction of stroke

Slant correction for a single stroke becomes complex as no headline can be assumed in a stroke. Headline is the defined area where end of each character is considered. In case of single character or stroke, no bottom line marks can be made. As defined earlier, character is a group of strokes; change in one stroke will change the shape of character. As such, chain code estimation method (Yimei et al., 2000) has been applied for slant correction in Gurmukhi characters. Fig. 3.6 shows how directions are considered in chain code estimation method.

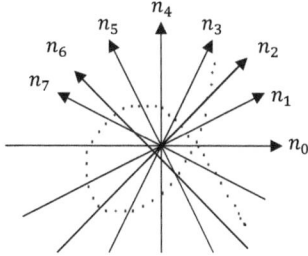

Fig. 3.6: Slant evaluation of stroke using 8-directional chain code method.

Slant correction algorithm contains the steps as given in Algorithm 3.4. In this algorithm, θ defines slant of stroke and n_j, $0 \leq j \leq 7$ are the chain elements in a stroke.

Algorithm 3.4

1. Set t = number of strokes in the list and set $k = 1$.
2. Repeat step 3 and step 4 for each stroke k, until $k \leq t$.
3.
    (a) Calculate m as the total number of points in current stroke k.
    (b) Calculate the number of chain elements $n_j, 0 \leq j \leq 7$ for stroke k.
    (c) Calculate slant of the stroke,
    $$\theta = \tan^{-1} \frac{(2 \times n_1 + 2 \times n_2 + n_3) - (n_5 + 2 \times n_6 + 2 \times n_7)}{(n_1 + 2 \times n_2 + 2 \times n_3) + 2 \times n_4 + (2 \times n_5 + 2 \times n_6 + n_7)}$$
4. If (($\theta > 45°$ and $\theta < 90°$) OR ($\theta > 90°$ and $\theta < 135°$)) then
    update x-coordinate of $P_i(x, y)$ as
    $$P_{i_x} = P_{i_x} + P_{i_y} \times \tan \theta \quad \forall \, i, 1 \leq i \leq m.$$
   End if
5. Set $k = k + 1$.
6. Exit.

Fig. 3.7 contains the character after smoothing and slant correction.

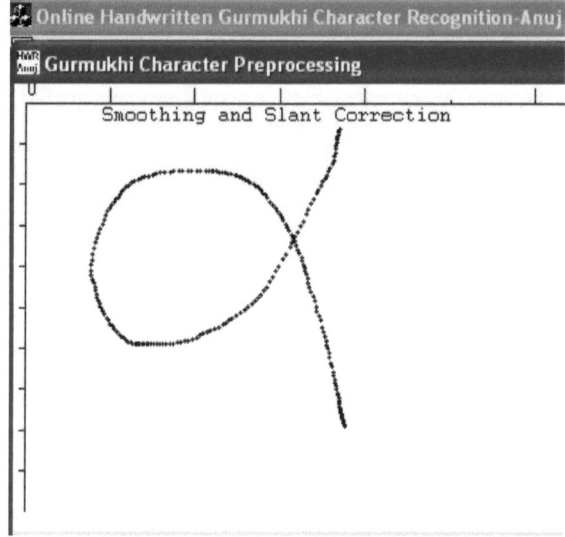

Fig. 3.7: Handwritten stroke after smoothing and slant correction.

3.5 Resampling of points in a stroke

Resampling of points is required to keep the points in the list at equal distances, as far as possible. For any pair of points in the list having a distance greater than one, we add a new point between such pairs. Any pair having distance less than one are untouched. The list obtained after the resampling of points is preprocessed. Fig. 3.8 shows the shape of stroke after applying the process of resampling of points. We have introduced one more step in resampling of points that filters the stroke points to fix the number of points in a stroke and also to retain the shape of stroke. Algorithm 3.5 consists of the steps of the process of resampling of points. In step 1, all the points in a list will be at the maximum distance of one with respect to their neighbouring points. In step 2, a filter is applied and fixed number of points are selected. Since any pair of points will be at a maximum distance of one after step 1, removal of points shall include two options: remove all points between pair of points having distance less than one, or, remove points at constant distances, *i.e.,* two or three and so on.

Algorithm 3.5

1. For all points in list,

    If((distance between two points) > 1) then

        call Algorithm 2.2 (interpolate missing points)

    End if

2. For all points of a stroke in a list, remove points at constant distance with respect to total number of points in a stroke.

3. Exit.

Fig. 3.8 contains the character after resampling of points.

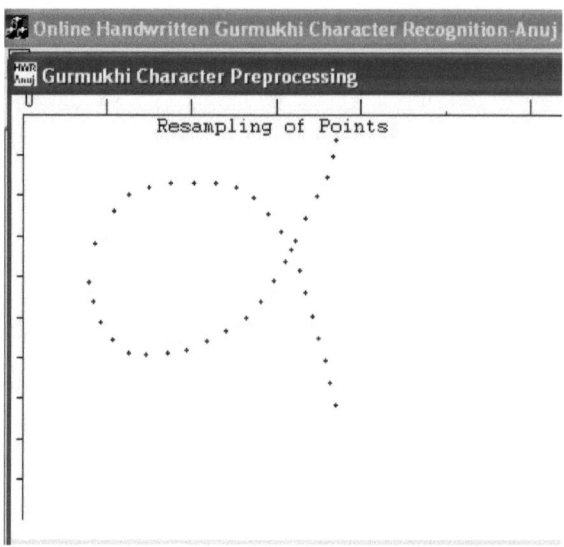

Fig. 3.8: Online handwritten stroke after resampling of points.

3.6 Preprocessing Source code

```cpp
// Preprocessing.cpp: implementation of the CPreprocessing class.
//

#include "stdafx.h"
#include "HWRAnuj.h"
#include "Stdlib.h"
#include "Graph.h"
//#include "Feature.h"
#include "OurConstants.h"
#include "Math.h"
#include "Preprocessing.h"

#ifdef _DEBUG
#undef THIS_FILE
static char THIS_FILE[]=__FILE__;
#define new DEBUG_NEW
#endif

// Construction/Destruction

CPreprocessing::CPreprocessing()
{
    m_FixedY = -200;
    m_xNor=200; m_yNor=-200;
    m_xTextLength=m_yTextLength=0; m_I=0; m_PPArray.RemoveAll();
}

CPreprocessing::~CPreprocessing()
{

}


double CPreprocessing::Round(double Value, int Precision)
{
    static const double Base = 10.0f;
    double Complete5, Complete5i;

    Complete5 = Value * pow(Base, (double) (Precision + 1));
    if (Value < 0.0f)
        Complete5 -= 5.0f;
    else
        Complete5 += 5.0f;
    Complete5 /= Base;
    modf(Complete5, &Complete5i);
    return Complete5i / pow(Base, (double) Precision);
}

double CPreprocessing::Distance(CPointNormalized& PrevPoint,
CPointNormalized& CurrPoint)
{
    return(Round(sqrt(pow((CurrPoint.x-PrevPoint.x),2) +
         pow((CurrPoint.y-PrevPoint.y),2)),2));
}
```

```cpp
double CPreprocessing::CalculateSlope(CPointNormalized& P1,
CPointNormalized& P2)
{
    if(P2.x!=P1.x)
        return(Round(((P2.y-P1.y)/(P2.x-P1.x)),2));
    else
        return -9999;    ///-9999 is for appx. 90 degree
}

void CPreprocessing::NonDecimalPoints()
{
    int i, Size;
    double fraction, t;
    CPointNormalized P;
    Size=m_PPArray.GetSize();
    for(i=0; i<Size; i++)
    {
        P=m_PPArray.GetAt(i);
        fraction=modf(P.x, &t);
        if(fraction>0.5) P.x=P.x+1-fraction;
        else P.x=P.x-fraction;
        fraction=modf(P.y, &t);
        if(fraction<-0.5) P.y=P.y-1-fraction;
        else P.y=P.y-fraction;
        m_PPArray.SetAt(i, P);
    }
}

void CPreprocessing::RoundPoints()
{
    int i, Size;
    CPointNormalized P;
    Size=m_PPArray.GetSize();
    for(i=0; i<Size; i++)
    {
        P=m_PPArray.GetAt(i);
        P.x=Round(P.x, 2); P.y=Round(P.y, 2);
        m_PPArray.SetAt(i, P);
    }
}

void CPreprocessing::RoundPointsZero()
{
    int i, Size;
    CPointNormalized P;
    Size=m_PPArray.GetSize();
    for(i=0; i<Size; i++)
    {
        P=m_PPArray.GetAt(i);
        P.x=Round(P.x, 0); P.y=Round(P.y, 0);
        m_PPArray.SetAt(i, P);
    }
}

void CPreprocessing::CreateTextFile(CString FileName)
{
```

```cpp
    int i, Size;
    CPointNormalized TempPoint;

    m_PPTextFile.Open(FileName, CFile::modeCreate |
    CFile::modeWrite);
    Size=m_PPArray.GetSize();
    if(Size>0)
    {
        for(i=0; i<Size; i++)
        {
            TempPoint = m_PPArray.GetAt(i);
            _gcvt_s(m_BufferX, 20, TempPoint.x,9);
m_PPTextFile.WriteString(m_BufferX);
            m_PPTextFile.WriteString(_T("\n"));
            _gcvt_s(m_BufferY, 20, TempPoint.y,9);
m_PPTextFile.WriteString(m_BufferY);
            m_PPTextFile.WriteString(_T("\n"));
        }
    }
    m_PPTextFile.Close();
}

void CPreprocessing::OriginalTextFilePoints()
{
    int i, Size;
    CPointNormalized TempPoint;
    Size=m_PPArray.GetSize();
    for(i=0; i<Size; i++)
    {
        TempPoint = m_PPArray.GetAt(i);
        TempPoint.y = (TempPoint.y-m_MaxY)-100;
        TempPoint.x = (TempPoint.x-m_MinX)+100;
        m_PPArray.SetAt(i, TempPoint);
    }
    RoundPoints();
}

void CPreprocessing::OriginalTextFile()
{
    m_FileName = "OriginalPoints.txt";
    //OriginalTextFilePoints();
    CreateTextFile(m_FileName);
}

void CPreprocessing::CalculateMaxMinText()
{
    int i, Size;
    CPointNormalized TempPoint;
    Size=m_PPArray.GetSize();
    xMax=0; xMin=300000; yMax=-300000; yMin=0;   //earlier in
Gurmukhi 3000, -3000
    for(i=0; i<Size; i++)
    {
        TempPoint = m_PPArray.GetAt(i);
        if(TempPoint.x > xMax)
            xMax = TempPoint.x;
        if(TempPoint.x < xMin)
```

```
                    xMin = TempPoint.x;
                if(TempPoint.y > yMax)
                    yMax = TempPoint.y;
                if(TempPoint.y < yMin)
                    yMin = TempPoint.y;
        }
        if(xMax>=fabs(yMin))
        {
            m_xFactor = (double)m_xNor/xMax;
        }
        else
        {
            m_yFactor = (double)m_yNor/yMin;
        }
        m_yxRatio=(double)fabs(yMin)/xMax;

}

void CPreprocessing::SizeNormalization()
{
        int i, Size;
        CPointNormalized TempPoint;
        Size=m_PPArray.GetSize();
        m_DiffX = fabs(m_MaxX-m_MinX); m_DiffY=fabs(m_MinY-m_MaxY);
        m_K = fabs(m_FixedY/m_DiffY);
        if(m_K>=20) m_K=1;
        //m_Ky = fabs(m_FixedY/m_DiffY);
        //m_K = fabs(m_DiffX/m_DiffY); m_NewXL = fabs(m_FixedY *
m_K); m_Kx = m_NewXL/m_DiffX;
        for(i=0; i<Size; i++)
        {
            TempPoint = m_PPArray.GetAt(i);
            TempPoint.y = (TempPoint.y-m_MaxY)*m_K; //earlier m_Ky
            TempPoint.x = (TempPoint.x-m_MinX)*m_K; //m_Kx, both
were same , replaced with m_K
            m_PPArray.SetAt(i, TempPoint);
        }
        RoundPoints();
}

void CPreprocessing::Centering()
{
        int i, Size;
        CPointNormalized TempPoint;
        Size=m_PPArray.GetSize();
        for(i=0; i<Size; i++)
        {
            if(m_xTextLength>=1000)
            {
                m_xTextLength=0;
                m_yTextLength+= m_yNor;
            }
            TempPoint = m_PPArray.GetAt(i);
            TempPoint.x += m_xTextLength;
            TempPoint.y += m_yTextLength;
            m_PPArray.SetAt(i, TempPoint);
```

```
        }
        m_xTextLength+=200;
}

void CPreprocessing::SizeCentering()
{
        m_FileName = "SizeCentering.txt";
        SizeNormalization();
        CreateTextFile(m_FileName);
}

void CPreprocessing::SizeCentering2()
{
        int i, Size; CPointNormalized TempPoint;
        Size=m_PPArray.GetSize();
        CalculateMaxMinText();
        m_xL=fabs(xMax-xMin);
        m_yL=fabs(yMin-yMax);
        if(m_xL<=200 && m_yL<=200)
        {
                for(i=0; i<Size; i++)
                {
                        TempPoint=m_PPArray.GetAt(i);
                        TempPoint.x -= xMin;
                        TempPoint.y -= yMax;
                        m_PPArray.SetAt(i, TempPoint);
                }
                if(m_xL > m_yL) m_Factor=200/m_xL;
                else m_Factor=200/m_yL;
                for(i=0; i<Size; i++)
                {
                        TempPoint=m_PPArray.GetAt(i);
                        TempPoint.x *= m_Factor;
                        TempPoint.y *= m_Factor;
                        m_PPArray.SetAt(i, TempPoint);
                }
        }

        RoundPoints();
}

void CPreprocessing::BSplineFormula(CPointNormalized& P1, CPointNormalized& P2,

        CPointNormalized& P3, CPointNormalized& P4)
{
        double mu;
        CPointNormalized P;
        for(mu=0; mu<=1; mu+=0.4)
        {
                P.x=((1-3*mu+3*mu*mu-mu*mu*mu)*P1.x + (3*mu*mu*mu-6*mu*mu+4)*P2.x +
                        (1+3*mu+3*mu*mu-3*mu*mu*mu)*P3.x +
(mu*mu*mu)*P4.x)/6;
                P.y=((1-3*mu+3*mu*mu-mu*mu*mu)*P1.y + (3*mu*mu*mu-6*mu*mu+4)*P2.y +
```

```
                    (1+3*mu+3*mu*mu-3*mu*mu*mu)*P3.y +
(mu*mu*mu)*P4.y)/6;
            P.strokeNumber=P1.strokeNumber;
            m_TempArray.SetAtGrow(m_I++, P);
        }
}

void CPreprocessing::UpdateArray()
{
        int i, Size;
        CPointNormalized P;
        m_PPArray.RemoveAll();
        Size=m_TempArray.GetSize();
        for(i=0;i<Size;i++)
        {
                P=m_TempArray.GetAt(i);
                m_PPArray.SetAtGrow(i, P);
        }
        m_TempArray.RemoveAll();
}

void CPreprocessing::BSpline()
{
        int i, Size;
        CPointNormalized P1, P2, P3, P4;
        m_TempArray.RemoveAll(); m_I=0;
        Size=m_PPArray.GetSize();
        if(Size>0)
        {
            m_TempArray.SetAtGrow(m_I++, m_PPArray.GetAt(0));
            for(i=0;i<(Size-3);i++)
            {
                    P1=m_PPArray.GetAt(i); P2=m_PPArray.GetAt(i+1);
                    P3=m_PPArray.GetAt(i+2); P4=m_PPArray.GetAt(i+3);
                    ///check for continous four points
                    if(P1.strokeNumber!=P2.strokeNumber)
                    {
                            m_TempArray.SetAtGrow(m_I++, P1);
                            m_TempArray.SetAtGrow(m_I++, P2);
                    }
                    else if(P1.strokeNumber!=P3.strokeNumber)
                    {
                            m_TempArray.SetAtGrow(m_I++, P1);
                    }
                    else if(P1.strokeNumber!=P4.strokeNumber)
                    {
                            m_TempArray.SetAtGrow(m_I++, P1);
                    }
                    else
                            BSplineFormula(P1, P2, P3, P4);
            }
///     } earlier in Gurmukhi
        m_TempArray.SetAtGrow(m_I++, m_PPArray.GetAt(Size-1));
        UpdateArray();
        }
}
```

```
void CPreprocessing::Interpolation()
{
    m_FileName = "BSpline.txt";
    BSpline();
    RoundPoints();
    CreateTextFile(m_FileName);
}

double CPreprocessing::FindStraightLine(int prev, int curr, int next)
{
    CPointNormalized Pprev, Pcurr, Pnext;
    Pprev=m_PPArray.GetAt(prev);
    Pcurr=m_PPArray.GetAt(curr); Pnext=m_PPArray.GetAt(next);
    return((pow(Distance(Pprev, Pcurr), 2)+pow(Distance(Pcurr, Pnext), 2)-
            pow(Distance(Pprev, Pnext), 2))/(2*Distance(Pprev, Pcurr)*Distance(Pprev, Pcurr)));
}

void CPreprocessing::EquiStraightLines()
{
    int prev, curr, next, Size;
    double val; m_I=0; m_TempArray.RemoveAll();
    prev=0; curr=prev+1; next=curr+1;
    Size=m_PPArray.GetSize();
    if(Size>0)
    {
        m_TempArray.SetAtGrow(m_I++, m_PPArray.GetAt(prev));
        while(next<=Size-1)
        {

    if(m_PPArray.GetAt(prev).strokeNumber==m_PPArray.GetAt(next).strokeNumber)
                {
                    val=FindStraightLine(prev, curr, next);
                    if((val > -1 && val < -0.90) || (val<1 && val>0.90))
                    {
                        if(Distance(m_PPArray.GetAt(prev), m_PPArray.GetAt(curr))>3)
                            m_TempArray.SetAtGrow(m_I++, m_PPArray.GetAt(curr));
                        prev=curr; curr=next; next=curr+1;
                    }
                    else
                    {
                        m_TempArray.SetAtGrow(m_I++, m_PPArray.GetAt(curr));
                        prev=curr; curr=prev+1; next=curr+1;
                    }
                    continue;
                }
                else
    if(m_PPArray.GetAt(prev).strokeNumber==m_PPArray.GetAt(curr).strokeNumber)
                {
```

```
                              m_TempArray.SetAtGrow(m_I++,
        m_PPArray.GetAt(prev));
                              m_TempArray.SetAtGrow(m_I++,
        m_PPArray.GetAt(curr));
                              m_TempArray.SetAtGrow(m_I++,
        m_PPArray.GetAt(next));
                              prev=next; curr=prev+1; next=curr+1;
                              continue;
                        }
                        else
                        {
                              m_TempArray.SetAtGrow(m_I++,
        m_PPArray.GetAt(prev));
                              m_TempArray.SetAtGrow(m_I++,
        m_PPArray.GetAt(curr));
                              prev=curr; curr=prev+1; next=curr+1;
                              continue;
                        }
                  }

            }
            UpdateArray(); NonDecimalPoints();
      }

      void CPreprocessing::FilterClosePoints()
      {
            m_FileName = "c:\\hwr\\AfterPP.txt";
      //    EquiStraightLines();
            NonDecimalPoints();
            CreateTextFile(m_FileName);
      }

      void CPreprocessing::EqualDistance(int From, int To)
      {
            double l, d=1;
            CPointNormalized P, P1, P2;
            P1=m_PPArray.GetAt(From); P2=m_PPArray.GetAt(To);
            l=fabs(Distance(P1, P2));
            while(l>d)
            {
                  P.strokeNumber=P1.strokeNumber;
                  P.x=(P1.x*(l-d)+P2.x*d)/l;
                  P.y=(P1.y*(l-d)+P2.y*d)/l;
                  m_TempArray.SetAtGrow(m_I++, P);
                  P1=P; l=fabs(Distance(P1, P2));
            }
            m_TempArray.SetAtGrow(m_I++, P2);
      }

      void CPreprocessing::EquiDistantPoints()
      {
            int i, j, k, Size, id, id2, N, Gap;
            m_I=0; m_TempArray.RemoveAll();
            Size=m_PPArray.GetSize();
            if(Size>0)
            {
                  m_TempArray.SetAtGrow(m_I++, m_PPArray.GetAt(0));
```

```
                for(i=0;i<Size-1;i++)
                {

        if(m_PPArray.GetAt(i).strokeNumber==m_PPArray.GetAt(i+1).str
okeNumber)
                        {
                                EqualDistance(i, i+1);
                        }
                        else
                                m_TempArray.SetAtGrow(m_I++,
m_PPArray.GetAt(i+1));
                }
                        m_TempArray.SetAtGrow(m_I++, m_PPArray.GetAt(i));
        }
        ///below code is for character with every stroke having
appx. 40 points only.
        m_TempArray2.RemoveAll();
        Size=m_TempArray.GetSize();
        j=0; i=0; id2=0;
        while(i<(Size))
        {
                if(

        //(m_TempArray.GetAt(i).strokeNumber!=m_TempArray.GetAt(i+1)
.strokeNumber) ||
                        (i+1)==Size)
                {
                        N=(i+1)-j; id=N/ARR_SIZE;
                        if(id>0)
                        {
                                Gap=N-(ARR_SIZE*id);
        /////First series to store
                                for(k=j; k<((N/2)-Gap)+j; k++)
                                {
                                        m_TempArray2.SetAtGrow(id2++,
m_TempArray.GetAt(k));
                                }
        ////Mid series to store
                                for(k=((N/2)-Gap)+j; k<((N/2)+Gap)+j;
k=k+2)
                                {
                                        m_TempArray2.SetAtGrow(id2++,
m_TempArray.GetAt(k));
                                }
        ////Last series to store
                                for(k=((N/2)+Gap)+j; k<=(i); k++)
                                {
                                        m_TempArray2.SetAtGrow(id2++,
m_TempArray.GetAt(k));
                                }
                        }
                        else
                        {
                                for(k=j; k<=(i); k++)
                                {
                                        m_TempArray2.SetAtGrow(id2++,
m_TempArray.GetAt(k));
```

```
                    }
                }
                j=i+1;
            }
            i++;
        }
        m_PPArray.RemoveAll();
    Size=m_TempArray2.GetSize();
    i=0; j=0; id2=0;
    while(i<(Size))
    {
        if(

//(m_TempArray2.GetAt(i).strokeNumber!=m_TempArray2.GetAt(i+
1).strokeNumber) ||
                (i+1)==Size)
            {
                N=(i+1)-j; id=N/ARR_SIZE;
                if(id>=1)
                {
                    for(k=j; k<(i+1); k=k+id)
                    {
                        m_PPArray.SetAtGrow(id2++,
m_TempArray2.GetAt(k));
                    }
                }
                else
                {
                    for(k=j; k<(i+1); k++)
                    {
                        m_PPArray.SetAtGrow(id2++,
m_TempArray2.GetAt(k));
                    }
                }
                if(k==Size-1)
                {
                    m_PPArray.SetAtGrow(id2++,
m_TempArray2.GetAt(k));
                }
                j=i+1;
            }
            i++;
    }
    /*
    while(i<(Size-1))
    {

    if((m_TempArray.GetAt(i).strokeNumber!=m_TempArray.GetAt(i+1
).strokeNumber) ||
                (i+1)==Size-1)
            {
                N=(i+1)-j; id=N/ARR_SIZE;
                if(id>0)
                {
                    Gap=N-(ARR_SIZE*id);
    /////First series to store
                    for(k=j; k<((N/2)-Gap)+j; k++)
```

```
                        {
                                m_TempArray2.SetAtGrow(id2++,
m_TempArray.GetAt(k));
                        }
        ////Mid series to store
                        for(k=((N/2)-Gap)+j; k<((N/2)+Gap)+j; k=k+2)
                        {
                                m_TempArray2.SetAtGrow(id2++,
m_TempArray.GetAt(k));
                        }
        ////Last series to store
                        for(k=((N/2)+Gap)+j; k<=(i+1); k++)
                        {
                                m_TempArray2.SetAtGrow(id2++,
m_TempArray.GetAt(k));
                        }
                    }
                    else
                    {
                        for(k=j; k<=(i+1); k++)
                        {
                                m_TempArray2.SetAtGrow(id2++,
m_TempArray.GetAt(k));
                        }
                    }
                    j=i+1;
            }
            i++;
    }
///finally store 40 points in a stroke
    m_PPArray.RemoveAll();
    Size=m_TempArray2.GetSize();
    i=0; j=0; id2=0;
    while(i<(Size-1))
    {
        if((m_TempArray2.GetAt(i).strokeNumber!=m_TempArray2.GetAt(i+1).strokeNumber) ||
                    (i+1)==Size-1)
            {
                N=(i+1)-j; id=N/ARR_SIZE;
                if(id>=1)
                {
                        for(k=j; k<(i+1); k=k+id)
                        {
                                m_PPArray.SetAtGrow(id2++,
m_TempArray2.GetAt(k));
                        }
                }
                else
                {
                        for(k=j; k<(i+1); k++)
                        {
                                m_PPArray.SetAtGrow(id2++,
m_TempArray2.GetAt(k));
                        }
```

```
                        }
                        if(k==Size-1)
                        {
                                m_PPArray.SetAtGrow(id2++,
    m_TempArray2.GetAt(k));
                        }
                        j=i+1;
                }
                i++;
        }

        /////
        //UpdateArray(); */
        RoundPoints();
}

void CPreprocessing::FilterSamePoints()
{
        int i=0, m_I=0, k=1, Size;
        CPointNormalized PPrev, PNext;
        m_TempArray.RemoveAll();
        Size=m_PPArray.GetSize();
        while(i<m_PPArray.GetUpperBound())
        {
                if((i+k)>m_PPArray.GetUpperBound())
                        break;
                PPrev=m_PPArray.GetAt(i);
                PNext=m_PPArray.GetAt(i+k);
                if(PPrev.x==PNext.x && PPrev.y==PNext.y)
                {
                        k++; continue;
                }
                else
                {
                        m_TempArray.SetAtGrow(m_I++, PPrev);
                        i=i+k; k=1;
                }
        //      i++;
        }
        m_TempArray.SetAtGrow(m_I++, PPrev);
        m_PPArray.RemoveAll(); m_I=0; i=0;
        while(i<=m_TempArray.GetUpperBound())
        {
                m_PPArray.SetAtGrow(m_I++, m_TempArray.GetAt(i));
                i++;
        }
        m_TempArray.RemoveAll();
}

void CPreprocessing::EquiDistantPointsNotFixed()
{
        int i, Size, Gap;
        m_I=0; m_TempArray.RemoveAll();
        Size=m_PPArray.GetSize();
        if(Size>0)
        {
                m_TempArray.SetAtGrow(m_I++, m_PPArray.GetAt(0));
```

```
            for(i=0;i<Size-1;i++)
            {

      if(m_PPArray.GetAt(i).strokeNumber==m_PPArray.GetAt(i+1).str
okeNumber)
                {
                        EqualDistance(i, i+1);
                }
                else
                        m_TempArray.SetAtGrow(m_I++,
m_PPArray.GetAt(i+1));
            }
            m_TempArray.SetAtGrow(m_I++, m_PPArray.GetAt(i));
      }
      m_PPArray.RemoveAll(); m_I=0; Size=m_TempArray.GetSize();
      m_pointsAfterPP = m_TempArray.GetSize();
      if(m_pointsBeforePP>0)       Gap =
(int)m_pointsAfterPP/m_pointsBeforePP;
      else Gap = (int)m_pointsAfterPP;
      i=0;
      if(Size>0)
      {
//     m_PPArray.SetAtGrow(m_I++, m_TempArray.GetAt(i));
            for(i=0;i<Size;i+=Gap)
            {
                  m_PPArray.SetAtGrow(m_I++, m_TempArray.GetAt(i));
            }
//     m_PPArray.SetAtGrow(m_I++, m_TempArray.GetAt(i));
      }
      m_TempArray.RemoveAll();
}

void CPreprocessing::Equidistancing()
{
      m_FileName = "EquiDistance.txt";
      if(ENGLISH==1)
            EquiDistantPointsNotFixed();
      else
            EquiDistantPoints();
      RoundPointsZero();
      FilterSamePoints();
      CreateTextFile(m_FileName);
//    FilterSamePoints();
//    EquiStraightLines(); RoundPoints(); UpdateArray();
      FilterClosePoints();
}

double CPreprocessing::GuassianFormulaX(double Mean, int From,
int To)
{
      int i, N;
      double StdDev=0;
      CPointNormalized P;
      N=(To-From)+1; Mean=Mean/N;
      for(i=From; i<=To; i++)
      {
            P=m_PPArray.GetAt(i);
```

```
            StdDev+=(P.x-Mean)*(P.x-Mean);
      }
      StdDev=StdDev/N;
      StdDev=sqrt(StdDev); StdDev=Round(StdDev, 2);
      return StdDev;
}

double CPreprocessing::GuassianFormulaY(double Mean, int From,
int To)
{
      int i, N;
      double StdDev=0;
      CPointNormalized P;
      N=(To-From)+1; Mean=Mean/N;
      for(i=From; i<=To; i++)
      {
            P=m_PPArray.GetAt(i);
            StdDev+=(P.y-Mean)*(P.y-Mean);
      }
      StdDev=StdDev/N;
      StdDev=sqrt(StdDev); StdDev=Round(StdDev, 2);
      return StdDev;
}

void CPreprocessing::GuassianArray(double K, double MeanX, double
MeanY, double StdDevX,
                                              double StdDevY, int
From, int To)
{
      int i;
      double e, gdf; ///pdf is guassian density function
      CPointNormalized P;
      MeanX=MeanY=(From-To)+1;
      for(i=From; i<=To; i++)
      {
            P=m_PPArray.GetAt(i);
            e=-1*(P.x-MeanX)*(P.x-MeanX)/(2*StdDevX*StdDevX);
            gdf=K*exp(e)/StdDevX;
            P.x=P.x+P.x*gdf; P.x=Round(P.x, 2);
            e=-1*(P.y-MeanY)*(P.y-MeanY)/(2*StdDevY*StdDevY);
            gdf=K*exp(e)/StdDevY;
            P.y=P.y+P.y*gdf; P.y=Round(P.y, 2);
            m_PPArray.SetAt(i, P);
      }
}

void CPreprocessing::GuassianSmoothing()
{
      int i, From=0, To, Size;
      double K, MeanX=0, MeanY=0, StdDevX, StdDevY;
      CPointNormalized P; m_I=0;
      Size=m_PPArray.GetSize();
      if(Size>0)
      {
            for(i=0;i<Size-1;i++)
            {
                  P=m_PPArray.GetAt(i);
```

```
            if(m_PPArray.GetAt(i).strokeNumber!=m_PPArray.GetAt(i+1).str
okeNumber)
                    {
                            To=i;
                            StdDevX=GuassianFormulaX(MeanX, From, To);
                            StdDevY=GuassianFormulaY(MeanY, From, To);
                            K=1/sqrt(2*3.14);
                            GuassianArray(K, MeanX, MeanY, StdDevX,
StdDevY, From, To);
                            From=i+1;
                    }
                    MeanX+=P.x; MeanY+=P.y;
            }
            To=Size-1;
            StdDevX=GuassianFormulaX(MeanX, From, To);
            StdDevY=GuassianFormulaY(MeanY, From, To);
            K=1/sqrt(2*3.14);
            GuassianArray(K, MeanX, MeanY, StdDevX, StdDevY, From,
To);
    }
}
void CPreprocessing::NeighbourMean(int i)
{
      CPointNormalized P, P1, P2;
      P=m_PPArray.GetAt(i);
      P1=m_PPArray.GetAt(i-1); P2=m_PPArray.GetAt(i+1);
      P.x=(P1.x+P2.x)/4+P.x/2;
      P.y=(P1.y+P2.y)/4+P.y/2;
      m_PPArray.SetAt(i, P);
}

void CPreprocessing::NeighbouringPoints()
{
      int i, Size;
      m_I=0;
      Size=m_PPArray.GetSize();
      if(Size>0)
      {
            for(i=1;i<Size-1;i++)
            {

      if(m_PPArray.GetAt(i).strokeNumber==m_PPArray.GetAt(i+1).str
okeNumber)
                    {
                            NeighbourMean(i);
                    }
                    else
                            i=i+1;
            }
      }
      RoundPoints();
}
void CPreprocessing::Smoothing()
{
```

65

```cpp
      m_FileName = "NbrPointSmooth.txt";
//    GuassianSmoothing();
      NeighbouringPoints();
      CreateTextFile(m_FileName);
}

double CPreprocessing::ChainCodeMethod(int From, int To)
{
      int i=0, Size, n0=0, n1=0, n2=0, n3=0;
      double m, theta;
      CPointNormalized Pi, Pj;
      Size=m_PPArray.GetSize();
      if(Size>0)
      {
            for(i=From;i<=To-3;i=i+3)
            {
      if(m_PPArray.GetAt(i).strokeNumber==m_PPArray.GetAt(i+3).str
okeNumber)
                  {
                        Pi=m_PPArray.GetAt(i);
Pj=m_PPArray.GetAt(i+3);
                        m=CalculateSlope(Pi, Pj);
                        if(m>-0.41 && m<=0.41)
                              n0++;
                        if(m>0.41 && m<=2.41)
                              n1++;
                        if(m>-2.41 && m<=-0.41)
                              n3++;
                        if(m>2.41)
                              n2++;
                        if(m<=-2.41)
                              n2++;
                  }//of if
                  else
                  {
                        continue;
                  }
            }
      }
      /*if((n1+n2+n3)==0)
            return 0;
      theta=((n1-n3)/(n1+n2+n3));*/
      if((n1+n2+n3)==0)
            return 0;
      theta=((double)(n1-n3)/(n1+n2+n3));
      theta=Round(theta, 2);
      return theta;
}

void CPreprocessing::UpdateSlant(int From, int To, double theta)
{
      int i;
      CPointNormalized P;
      for(i=From;i<=To;i++)
      {
            P=m_PPArray.GetAt(i);
```

```cpp
            P.x=P.x-P.y*theta;
            P.x=Round(P.x, 2); P.y=Round(P.y, 2);
            m_TempArray.SetAtGrow(m_I++, P);
      }
}

void CPreprocessing::SlantAdjustment(int From, int To)
{
      int i; double AdjustX;
      CPointNormalized P;
      AdjustX=m_PPArray.GetAt(From).x-m_TempArray.GetAt(From).x;
      for(i=From; i<=To; i++)
      {
            P=m_TempArray.GetAt(i);
            P.x=P.x+AdjustX;
            m_TempArray.SetAt(i, P);
      }
}

void CPreprocessing::SlantCorrectionMethod()
{
      int i=0, From=0, To, Size;
      double AdjustX, theta=0;
      m_I=0; Size=m_PPArray.GetSize();
      To=Size-1; AdjustX=m_PPArray.GetAt(From).x;
      bool wholeWordSlant = true; //required for finding slant of whole word and not individual strokes
      if(Size>0)
      {
            if(wholeWordSlant){
                  theta=ChainCodeMethod(From, To);
                  UpdateSlant(From, To, theta);
                  SlantAdjustment(From, To);
            }
            else{
            for(i=0;i<m_PPArray.GetUpperBound(); i++)
            {

      if(m_PPArray.GetAt(i).strokeNumber!=m_PPArray.GetAt(i+1).strokeNumber ||
                        i==m_PPArray.GetUpperBound()-1)
                  {
                        To=i;
                        theta=ChainCodeMethod(From, To);
                        UpdateSlant(From, To, theta);
                        SlantAdjustment(From, To);
                        From=i+1;
                  }
            }
            }//else
            UpdateArray();
      }
}

void CPreprocessing::SlantCorrection()
{
      m_FileName = "SlantCorrection.txt";
```

```cpp
        SlantCorrectionMethod();
        RoundPoints();
        CreateTextFile(m_FileName);
}

int CPreprocessing::AddToPPList(CList<CPoint, const CPoint&>* pPointList)
{
        CPoint Point, PrevPoint; m_MinX=200000; m_MaxX=0; m_MinY=0; m_MaxY=-200000;// for word R
        CPointNormalized PointRecord;
//      CFeature ObjFeature;
        int i=0, SI=1; m_PPArray.RemoveAll();
        POSITION aPos = pPointList->GetHeadPosition();
        if(aPos)
        {
                while(aPos)
                {
                        Point = pPointList->GetNext(aPos);
                        if(Point.y > 0)
                        {
                                SI++;
                                continue;
                        }
                        ///for WordR
                        if(Point.x<m_MinX) m_MinX=Point.x;
                        if(Point.x>m_MaxX) m_MaxX=Point.x;
                        if(Point.y<m_MinY) m_MinY=Point.y;
                        if(Point.y>m_MaxY) m_MaxY=Point.y;
                        ////
                        PointRecord.x = Point.x;
                        PointRecord.y = Point.y;
                        PointRecord.strokeNumber = SI;
                        m_PPArray.SetAtGrow(i++, PointRecord);
                        PrevPoint = Point;
                }
        }
        m_pointsBeforePP = m_PPArray.GetSize();
        RoundPoints();
        OriginalTextFile();
        SizeCentering();
        Interpolation();
        Smoothing();
        SlantCorrection();
        Equidistancing();
//      ObjFeature.ExtractFeatures(&m_PPArray);
        return 1;
}
```

CHAPTER 4

PREPROCESSING GRAPH INTERFACE

4.1 Source Code to Display Preprocessed Strokes

///Graph

```cpp
// Graph.cpp: implementation of the CGraph class.

#include "stdafx.h"
#include "GraphDialog.h"
#include "Math.h"
#include "Stdlib.h"
#include "String.h"
#include "HWRAnuj.h"
#include "Graph.h"

#ifdef _DEBUG
#undef THIS_FILE
static char THIS_FILE[]=__FILE__;
#define new DEBUG_NEW
#endif

// Construction/Destruction

#pragma warning (disable:4244 4018 4701)

CGraph::CGraph()
{
    GraphSetAllDefaults();

}

CGraph::CGraph(CWnd *pParentWnd, int xPos, int yPos, int Width, int Height, UINT colorscheme)
{
    GraphSetAllDefaults();

    //setup default values
    m_pWnd=pParentWnd;
    SetColorScheme(colorscheme);
    //set graph position
    m_iGraphX=xPos<0?0:xPos;
    m_iGraphY=yPos<0?0:yPos;
    //set graphsize (0 or less means default)
    m_iGraphWidth = Width <
G_MINGRAPHWIDTH?G_MINGRAPHWIDTH:Width;
```

```
      m_iGraphHeight=Height < G_MINGRAPHHEIGHT
?G_MINGRAPHHEIGHT:Height;


}
CGraph::~CGraph()
{
//    graphTextFile.Close();
}


//////////
void CGraph::GraphSetAllDefaults()
{
      //setup default values
      m_pWnd=NULL;
      //create default font
      CreateGraphFont("Courier",8);
      SetDefaultColorScheme();
      m_bAutofit=TRUE;
      m_bShowGrid=TRUE;
      m_bShowTicks=TRUE;
      m_bYLineAtLeft=FALSE;
      //set default graph position
      m_iGraphX=0;
      m_iGraphY=0;
      //set default graph size
      SetGraphSizePos(0, 0,G_MINGRAPHWIDTH,G_MINGRAPHHEIGHT);
      //set the axis scaling
      SetXAxisScale(G_DEFAULTXMIN,G_DEFAULTXMAX);
      SetYAxisScale(G_DEFAULTYMIN,G_DEFAULTYMAX);
      //set the legend and Title Texts
      SetDefaultGraphTitle();
      SetDefaultXLegend();
      SetDefaultYLegend();
      SetDefaultFunctionName();

      //other stuff
      m_pFunctionParams=NULL;
}

//
void CGraph::SetColorScheme(int Scheme, BOOL bRedraw)
{
      switch (Scheme)
      {
      case G_DEFAULTSCHEME:
            break;
      case G_WHITESCHEME:
            m_crYTickColor=RGB(0,0,0);
            m_crXTickColor=RGB(0,0,0);
            m_crYLegendTextColor=RGB(0,0,0);
            m_crXLegendTextColor=RGB(0,0,0);
            m_crGraphTitleColor=RGB(0,0,0);
            m_crGraphPenColor=RGB(0,0,0);
            m_crGraphBkColor=RGB(255,255,255);//RGB(192,192,192);-
-gray
```

```
            m_crFunctionNameColor=RGB(0,0,0);
            m_crGridColor=RGB(220,220,220);
            break;
      case G_REDSCHEME:
            m_crYTickColor=RGB(255,255,255);
            m_crXTickColor=RGB(255,255,255);
            m_crYLegendTextColor=RGB(255,200,200);
            m_crXLegendTextColor=RGB(255,150,150);
            m_crGraphTitleColor=RGB(255,255,255);
            m_crGraphPenColor=RGB(255,255,0);
            m_crGraphBkColor=RGB(128,0,0);
            m_crFunctionNameColor=RGB(255,0,0);
            m_crGridColor=RGB(200,0,0);
            break;
      case G_BLUESCHEME:
            m_crYTickColor=RGB(255,255,0);
            m_crXTickColor=RGB(255,255,0);
            m_crYLegendTextColor=RGB(200,200,255);
            m_crXLegendTextColor=RGB(150,150,255);
            m_crGraphTitleColor=RGB(255,255,255);
            m_crGraphPenColor=RGB(0,255,255);
            m_crGraphBkColor=RGB(0,0,128);
            m_crFunctionNameColor=RGB(0,0,255);
            m_crGridColor=RGB(0,0,200);
            break;
      case G_GREENSCHEME:
            m_crYTickColor=RGB(255,255,255);
            m_crXTickColor=RGB(255,255,255);
            m_crYLegendTextColor=RGB(200,255,200);
            m_crXLegendTextColor=RGB(150,255,150);
            m_crGraphTitleColor=RGB(0,255,255);
            m_crGraphPenColor=RGB(255,255,255);
            m_crGraphBkColor=RGB(0,128,0);
            m_crFunctionNameColor=RGB(255,0,255);
            m_crGridColor=RGB(0,200,0);
            break;
      case G_CYANSCHEME:
            m_crYTickColor=RGB(255,0,255);
            m_crXTickColor=RGB(255,0,255);
            m_crYLegendTextColor=RGB(200,255,200);
            m_crXLegendTextColor=RGB(150,255,150);
            m_crGraphTitleColor=RGB(192,192,192);
            m_crGraphPenColor=RGB(255,255,0);
            m_crGraphBkColor=RGB(0,128,128);
            m_crFunctionNameColor=RGB(255,255,255);
            m_crGridColor=RGB(0,64,64);
            break;
      case G_YELLOWSCHEME:
            m_crYTickColor=RGB(0,255,255);
            m_crXTickColor=RGB(0,255,255);
            m_crYLegendTextColor=RGB(200,200,0);
            m_crXLegendTextColor=RGB(255,255,0);
            m_crGraphTitleColor=RGB(192,192,192);
            m_crGraphPenColor=RGB(192,192,192);
            m_crGraphBkColor=RGB(128,128,0);
            m_crFunctionNameColor=RGB(255,255,255);
            m_crGridColor=RGB(0,64,64);
```

```cpp
                break;
        case G_MAGENTASCHEME:
                m_crYTickColor=RGB(192,192,255);
                m_crXTickColor=RGB(100,100,255);
                m_crYLegendTextColor=RGB(255,0,0);
                m_crXLegendTextColor=RGB(255,128,128);
                m_crGraphTitleColor=RGB(128,255,128);
                m_crGraphPenColor=RGB(255,255,255);
                m_crGraphBkColor=RGB(128,0,128);
                m_crFunctionNameColor=RGB(255,255,192);
                m_crGridColor=RGB(192,0,192);
                break;
        default:
                break;

        }
        if(bRedraw)
        {
                PaintGraph();
        }
}

void CGraph::CreateGraphFont(CString FaceName, UINT size)
{

        CFont *poldfont;
        HDC hDC;
        CDC *dc;
        TEXTMETRIC textmetrics;
        if (!m_pWnd)//if we don't have a holding window
        {
                hDC=GetDC(0);//get a whole screen dc
                dc=new CDC;
                dc->Attach(hDC);
        }
        else
        {
                dc=m_pWnd->GetDC();
        }

        //detach old font if any
        m_GraphFont.Detach();
        //create the new one
        m_GraphFont.CreatePointFont(size*10,FaceName,dc);

        poldfont=dc->SelectObject(&m_GraphFont);

        dc->GetTextMetrics(&textmetrics);
        m_iCharHeight=textmetrics.tmHeight;
        m_iCharWidth=textmetrics.tmAveCharWidth;

        dc->SelectObject(poldfont);
        if(!m_pWnd)
        {
                dc->Detach();
                ReleaseDC(0,hDC);
                delete dc;
```

```
    }
    else
    {
        m_pWnd->ReleaseDC(dc);
    }

    m_iFontSize=size;
    m_szFontFace=FaceName;

    //we need to rescale the graph
    SetXAxisScale(m_dXAxisMin, m_dXAxisMax);
    SetYAxisScale(m_dYAxisMin, m_dYAxisMax);
}

void CGraph::SetGraphSizePos(int xPos, int yPos, int Width, int Height)
{
    CRect rect;
    rect.left=m_iGraphX;
    rect.top=m_iGraphY;
    rect.right=rect.left+m_iGraphWidth;
    rect.bottom=rect.top+m_iGraphHeight;

    m_iGraphX=xPos < 0?m_iGraphX:xPos;
    m_iGraphY=yPos < 0?m_iGraphY:yPos;

    Width= (Width>0 && Width <G_MINGRAPHWIDTH)?G_MINGRAPHWIDTH:Width;
    m_iGraphWidth = Width <= 0? m_iGraphWidth :Width;

    Height = (Height>0 && Height <G_MINGRAPHHEIGHT)?G_MINGRAPHHEIGHT:Height;
    m_iGraphHeight = Height <= 0? m_iGraphHeight : Height;

    //remember to rescale the graph
    SetXAxisScale(m_dXAxisMin,m_dXAxisMax);
    SetYAxisScale(m_dYAxisMin,m_dYAxisMax);

    //clear old graph from the screen
    if(m_pWnd)
    {
        m_pWnd->InvalidateRect(&rect,TRUE);
        m_pWnd->SendMessage(WM_PAINT,0,0);
    }
}

UINT CGraph::CalcTopMargin()
{
    return 1*m_iCharHeight;
}


UINT CGraph::CalcBottomMargin()
{
    return 1*m_iCharHeight;
}
```

```
UINT CGraph::CalcLeftMargin()
{
      return 1*m_iCharWidth;
}

UINT CGraph::CalcRightMargin()
{
      return m_iCharWidth;
}

void CGraph::SetXAxisScale(double min, double max)
{
      //swap min and max if they are the wrong way around
      double temp,scale;
      if (max < min)
      {
            temp =min;
            min=max;
            max=temp;
      }
      if(min==max)
      {
            max+= 0.1;
      }


      //set the member variables
      m_dXAxisMax=max;
      m_dXAxisMin=min;
      //
      UINT lmargin=CalcLeftMargin();
      UINT rmargin=CalcRightMargin();

      if (m_bAutofit) //Autofit is always true @ 26 Feb 2005
      {
            temp=max-min;//the spread of the x-axiz
            scale=(m_iGraphWidth-lmargin-rmargin)/temp;//calc pixels/x
            m_dPixelsPerX=scale;
      }
      else
      {
            m_dPixelsPerX=1;//1:1
      }

      //where would the x-origin be located?
      if( (min < 0) && (max >0))
      {
            m_iOriginX=abs(min) * m_dPixelsPerX + lmargin;
      }
      else if ( (min <0) && (max <=0))
      {
            m_iOriginX=(m_iGraphWidth)-rmargin;
      }
      else if (min >=0 && (max>=0))
      {
```

```
            m_iOriginX=lmargin;
      }
}


void CGraph::SetYAxisScale(double min, double max)
{
      double temp,scale;
      //swap min and max if they are the wrong way around
      if (max < min)
      {
            temp=min;
            min=max;
            max=temp;
      }

      if(min==max)
      {
            max+= 0.1;
      }

      //set the member variables
      m_dYAxisMin=min;
      m_dYAxisMax=max;

      //calculate scaling
      UINT bmargin=CalcBottomMargin();
      UINT tmargin=CalcTopMargin();
      CRect dataarea=CalcDataArea();

      if (m_bAutofit)//Always TRUE as at 26/02/2005
      {
            temp=max-min;//the spread of the y-axiz
            scale=(m_iGraphHeight-(bmargin+tmargin))/temp;//calc pixels/x
            m_dPixelsPerY=scale;
      }
      else
      {
            m_dPixelsPerY=1;//1:1
      }

      //where should the Y origin be?

      if (min<0 && max >0)//if Y passes through zero
      {
            //from the bottom of the graph
            m_iOriginY=abs(min)*m_dPixelsPerY+bmargin;
      }
      else if(min<0 && max<=0)//if Y values are all negative
      {
            m_iOriginY=(dataarea.bottom-dataarea.top)+bmargin;
      }
      else if (min >=0 && max >=0)//if Y values are all positive
      {
            m_iOriginY=bmargin;
      }
```

```
}

void CGraph::PaintGraph()
{
      if (m_pWnd==NULL)
      {
            return;
      }
      CRect rect;
      CPen pen, *oldpen;
      CDC *dc=m_pWnd->GetDC();
      UINT lmargin=CalcLeftMargin();
      UINT rmargin=CalcRightMargin();
      UINT bmargin=CalcBottomMargin();
      UINT tmargin=CalcTopMargin();
      UINT Graphbottom=m_iGraphY+m_iGraphHeight;
      UINT Graphright=m_iGraphX+m_iGraphWidth;
      UINT Graphtop=m_iGraphX;UINT Graphleft=m_iGraphX;//

      CBrush brush,*poldbrush;
      brush.CreateSolidBrush(m_crGraphBkColor);
      pen.CreatePen(PS_SOLID,1,m_crGraphBkColor);
      rect.left=m_iGraphX;
      rect.right =rect.left+m_iGraphWidth;
      rect.top=m_iGraphY;
      rect.bottom=rect.top+m_iGraphHeight;
      oldpen=dc->SelectObject(&pen);
      poldbrush=dc->SelectObject(&brush);
      dc->Rectangle(&rect);
      dc->SelectObject(oldpen);
      dc->SelectObject(poldbrush);
      pen.Detach();

      dc->MoveTo(m_iGraphX+lmargin,Graphleft+tmargin);
      pen.CreatePen(PS_SOLID,1,m_crXTickColor);
      oldpen=dc->SelectObject(&pen);
      dc->LineTo(Graphright+rmargin,Graphleft+tmargin);
      dc->SelectObject(oldpen);
      pen.Detach();

      //draw the Y Axis
      pen.CreatePen(PS_SOLID,1,m_crXTickColor);
      oldpen=dc->SelectObject(&pen);
      if (!m_bYLineAtLeft)
      {
            dc->MoveTo(m_iGraphX+lmargin,Graphleft+bmargin);
            dc->LineTo(m_iGraphX+m_iOriginX,Graphbottom-bmargin);
      }
      else
      {
            dc->MoveTo(m_iGraphX+lmargin,Graphleft+bmargin);
            dc->LineTo(m_iGraphX+lmargin,Graphbottom-bmargin);
      }
      dc->SelectObject(oldpen);
      pen.Detach();
```

```
        DrawTicks();
        DrawGraphTitle();
        DrawXAxisNumbers();
        DrawYAxisNumbers();
        DrawFunction();

}

void CGraph::DrawTicks()
{
        if (!m_pWnd)
        {
             return;
        }
        if (!m_bShowTicks)
        {
             return;
        }
        CPen TickPen, *poldpen;
        UINT bmargin=CalcBottomMargin();
        CRect dataarea=CalcDataArea();
        //UINT GraphBottom=m_iGraphY+m_iGraphHeight;
        UINT GraphBottom=m_iGraphY+bmargin;//+m_iGraphHeight;

        CDC *pdc=m_pWnd->GetDC();
        //start with the x-axis
        TickPen.CreatePen(PS_SOLID,1,m_crXTickColor);
        poldpen=pdc->SelectObject(&TickPen);
        double GridSpacing=CalcXAxisGridAndTicks();
        UINT xtoptick=((GraphBottom-m_iOriginY)-dataarea.top <
G_TICKLENGTH/2)?(GraphBottom-m_iOriginY)-
dataarea.top:G_TICKLENGTH/2;
        UINT xbottick=(dataarea.bottom-(GraphBottom-m_iOriginY)
<G_TICKLENGTH/2)?dataarea.bottom-(GraphBottom-
m_iOriginY):G_TICKLENGTH/2;
        xbottick=xbottick/4;
        int n;
        for(n=1;n<G_NUMTICKSANDGRID;n++)
        {
             pdc->MoveTo(dataarea.left+n*GridSpacing,GraphBottom-10);
             pdc->LineTo(dataarea.left+n*GridSpacing,GraphBottom-xtoptick);
             //bottom ticks
             pdc->LineTo(dataarea.left+n*GridSpacing,GraphBottom+xbottick);

        }

        //now do the x axis ticks
        pdc->SelectObject(poldpen);
        TickPen.Detach();
        TickPen.CreatePen(PS_SOLID,1,m_crYTickColor);
        poldpen=pdc->SelectObject(&TickPen);
        GridSpacing=CalcYAxisGridAndTicks();
```

```
        UINT ylefttick=( (m_iGraphX+m_iOriginX)-dataarea.left
<G_TICKLENGTH/2)? (m_iGraphX+m_iOriginX)-
dataarea.left:G_TICKLENGTH/2;
        UINT yrighttick=( dataarea.right-(m_iGraphX+m_iOriginX)
<G_TICKLENGTH/2)? dataarea.right-
(m_iGraphX+m_iOriginX):G_TICKLENGTH/2;
        //check for the special case where the y-axis has been
forced to the left
        if(m_bYLineAtLeft)
        {
                ylefttick=0;
        }

        int x,y;
        if(m_bYLineAtLeft)
        {
                x=dataarea.left;
                y=dataarea.bottom;
        }
        else
        {
                x=m_iGraphX+m_iOriginX;
                y=dataarea.bottom;
        }


        for(n=1;n<G_NUMTICKSANDGRID;n++)
        {
                //Loop and do the y axis ticks

                pdc->MoveTo(x,y-(n*GridSpacing));
                //do left side tick
                pdc->LineTo(x-ylefttick,y-(n*GridSpacing));
                //do rightside tick
                pdc->LineTo(x-yrighttick,y-(n*GridSpacing));
        }

        //cleanup
        pdc->SelectObject(poldpen);
        m_pWnd->ReleaseDC(pdc);
}


CRect CGraph::CalcDataArea()
{
        CRect dataarea;
        dataarea.left=m_iGraphX+CalcLeftMargin();
        dataarea.right=m_iGraphX+m_iGraphWidth-CalcRightMargin();
        dataarea.top=m_iGraphY+CalcTopMargin();
        dataarea.bottom=m_iGraphY+m_iGraphHeight-CalcBottomMargin();
        return dataarea;
}

double CGraph::CalcXAxisGridAndTicks()
{
        //the placing of the ticks co-incide with gridlines
        CRect rect=CalcDataArea();
```

```
       return ((double)rect.right-
(double)rect.left)/(double)G_NUMTICKSANDGRID;

}

double CGraph::CalcYAxisGridAndTicks()
{
       //the placing of the ticks co-incide with gridlines
       CRect rect=CalcDataArea();
       return ((double)rect.bottom-
(double)rect.top)/(double)G_NUMTICKSANDGRID;
}


void CGraph::DrawGraphTitle()
{
       if (m_pWnd==NULL)
       {
              return;
       }
       UINT lmargin=CalcLeftMargin();
       UINT rmargin=CalcRightMargin();
       CRect rect;
       rect.left=10;//rect.left=m_iGraphX+lmargin;
       rect.top=14;//rect.top=m_iGraphHeight+m_iCharHeight;
       rect.right=350;//rect.right=m_iGraphX+m_iGraphWidth-rmargin;
       rect.bottom=40;//rect.bottom=rect.top+m_iCharHeight;
       CDC *pdc=m_pWnd->GetDC();
       CFont *poldfont;

       CBrush brush;
       brush.CreateSolidBrush(m_crGraphBkColor);
       pdc->FillRect(&rect,&brush);

       pdc->SetBkMode(TRANSPARENT);
       pdc->SetTextColor(m_crGraphTitleColor);
       poldfont=pdc->SelectObject(&m_GraphFont);
       pdc-
>DrawText(m_szGraphTitle,&rect,DT_CENTER|DT_END_ELLIPSIS);

       //cleanup
       pdc->SelectObject(poldfont);
       m_pWnd->ReleaseDC(pdc);
}

void CGraph::DrawXAxisNumbers()
{
       if (!m_pWnd)
       {
              return;
       }
       CString astring;
       CRect rect,dataarea;
       CFont *poldfont;
       CDC *pdc;

       pdc=m_pWnd->GetDC();
```

```
        poldfont=pdc->SelectObject(&m_GraphFont);
        pdc->SetTextColor(m_crXLegendTextColor);
        pdc->SetBkMode(TRANSPARENT);

        dataarea=CalcDataArea();
        rect.left=dataarea.left;
        rect.top=m_iGraphY-CalcTopMargin()/3;
        rect.right=rect.left+5*m_iCharWidth;
        rect.bottom=rect.top+m_iCharHeight;
        rect.top+=1;
        rect.bottom+=1;
        //clear any old text
        CBrush brush;
        brush.CreateSolidBrush(m_crGraphBkColor);
        pdc->FillRect(&rect,&brush);
        //format and print the number
        astring.Format("%.4g",m_dXAxisMin);
        pdc->DrawText(astring,&rect,DT_NOCLIP|DT_LEFT);
        rect.left=dataarea.left+((dataarea.right-dataarea.left)/2);
        rect.left=rect.left-4*m_iCharWidth;
        rect.right=rect.left+8*m_iCharWidth;
        rect.top+=1;
        rect.bottom+=1;
        pdc->FillRect(&rect,&brush);
        astring.Format("%.4g",(m_dXAxisMin+m_dXAxisMax)/2);
        rect.left=dataarea.right-8*m_iCharWidth;
        rect.right=dataarea.right;
        rect.top+=1;
        rect.bottom+=1;
        pdc->FillRect(&rect,&brush);
        astring.Format("%.4g",m_dXAxisMax);// note the lack of - in
the format
        pdc->DrawText(astring,&rect,DT_NOCLIP|DT_RIGHT);

        //cleanup
        pdc->SelectObject(poldfont);


}


void CGraph::DrawYAxisNumbers()
{
        if(!m_pWnd)
        {
                return;
        }
        CString astring;
        CRect rect,dataarea;
        CFont *poldfont;
        CDC *pdc;

        pdc=m_pWnd->GetDC();
        poldfont=pdc->SelectObject(&m_GraphFont);
        pdc->SetTextColor(m_crYLegendTextColor);
        pdc->SetBkMode(TRANSPARENT);
```

```
        dataarea=CalcDataArea();
        CBrush brush;
        rect.left=m_iGraphX+2*m_iCharWidth;
rect.right=rect.left+5*m_iCharWidth;
        brush.CreateSolidBrush(m_crGraphBkColor);
        //do the max value
        rect.top=dataarea.bottom-m_iCharHeight;
        rect.bottom=rect.top+m_iCharHeight;
        rect.DeflateRect(0,0,1,0);
        pdc->FillRect(&rect,&brush);
        astring.Format("%.4g",(m_dYAxisMin));
        pdc->SelectObject(poldfont);
}

void CGraph::SetDefaultColorScheme()
{
        SetColorScheme(G_BLUESCHEME);
}


void CGraph::SetDefaultGraphTitle()
{
        m_szGraphTitle="Graph Title goes here";
}


void CGraph::SetDefaultXLegend()
{
        m_szXLegendText="X Axis Legend Text here";
}

void CGraph::SetDefaultYLegend()
{
        m_szYLegendText="Y Axis Legend text  here";
}

void CGraph::SetDefaultFunctionName()
{
        m_szFunctionNameText="Function Name (or extra text)";
}


void CGraph::SetGraphTitle(CString GraphTitle)
{
        m_szGraphTitle=GraphTitle;
        DrawGraphTitle();

}


void CGraph::SetXLegendText(CString XText)
{
        m_szXLegendText=XText;
        DrawXLegend();
}
```

```
void CGraph::SetYLegendText(CString YText)
{
    m_szYLegendText=YText;
    DrawYLegend();
}


void CGraph::SetFunctionName(CString FunctionName)
{
    m_szFunctionNameText=FunctionName;
    DrawFunctionName();
}



void CGraph::SetYLineAtLeft(BOOL AtLeft)
{
    BOOL bprevious=m_bYLineAtLeft;
    m_bYLineAtLeft=AtLeft;
    //if there is a change in the Y line position then we will have to
    //redraw the graph
    if (m_bYLineAtLeft != bprevious)
    {
        PaintGraph();
    }
}

void CGraph::ShowGrid(BOOL bShow)
{
    //this is public function
    //show the graph grid if bShow==TRUE
    //or vice-versa
    BOOL bprevious=m_bShowGrid;
    m_bShowGrid=bShow;
    //if there is a change then repaint
    if (m_bShowGrid !=bprevious)
    {
        PaintGraph();
    }
}

void CGraph::ShowTicks(BOOL bShow)
{
    BOOL bprevious=m_bShowTicks;
    m_bShowTicks=bShow;
    if (m_bShowTicks!=bprevious)
    {
        PaintGraph();
    }

}

LONG CGraph::ConvertToGraphCoords(double x, double y)
{
    LONG result =-1;
```

```
        if(x < m_dXAxisMin || x > m_dXAxisMax)
        {
                return result;
        }
        if( y <m_dYAxisMin || y > m_dYAxisMax)
        {
                return result;
        }
        double xdif = abs(m_dXAxisMin - x);
        double ydif = abs(m_dYAxisMin - y);

        CRect rect=CalcDataArea();

         int xpos=rect.left+(xdif*m_dPixelsPerX); //from left
        int ypos=rect.bottom-(ydif*m_dPixelsPerY); //from bottom

        result=MAKELONG(xpos,ypos);

        return result;
}


BOOL CGraph::DoFunction(G_FUNCTIONSTRUCT *pFunctionParams)
{
        m_pFunctionParams=pFunctionParams;
        SetGraphTitle(m_pFunctionParams->szGraphTitle);
        SetXLegendText(m_pFunctionParams->szXLegend);
        SetYLegendText(m_pFunctionParams->szYLegend);
        SetFunctionName((CString)"function: Curve of drawn Pen
movement");

        double xminimum;
        xminimum=pFunctionParams->xMin;

        SetXAxisScale(xminimum,pFunctionParams->xMax);
        SetYAxisScale(pFunctionParams->yMin,pFunctionParams->yMax);

        PaintGraph();
        return TRUE;
}
void CGraph::ClearFunction()
{
        m_pFunctionParams=NULL; //reset the pointer
        //Clear the graph
        PaintGraph();
}
void CGraph::DrawFunction()
{
        CDC* pDC;pDC = m_pWnd->GetDC();
        if(!m_pWnd)
        {
                return;
        }

        if(!m_pFunctionParams)
        {
```

```
//      pDC->TextOut(250,250,"m_pFunctionParams not null");
        return;
    }

    DoCurve();

}

void CGraph::AddToFloatList(double xFloat, double yFloat)
{
    CFloatPoint FloatPoint;
    FloatPoint.xFloat = xFloat;
    FloatPoint.yFloat = yFloat;
    m_graphPointList.AddTail(FloatPoint);
}

void CGraph::DoCurve()
{
    CString xstr1,ystr1,pathName;
    CFloatPoint FloatPoint;
    switch(m_GraphType)
    {
    case 1:
        pathName="OriginalPoints.txt";
        break;
    case 2:
        pathName="SizeCentering.txt";
        break;
    case 3:
        pathName="BSpline.txt";
        break;
    case 4:
        pathName="NbrPointSmooth.txt";
        break;
    case 5:
        pathName="SlantCorrection.txt";
        break;
    case 6:

    pathName="C:\\hwr_data\\2_Characters\\2_pp\\pp_49.dat";
        break;
    case 7:
        pathName="EquiDistance.txt";
        break;
    default:
        pathName="AfterPP.txt";
        break;
    }

    if(!m_graphPointList.IsEmpty())
    {
        m_graphPointList.RemoveAll();
    }

    if(m_GraphType==6)
    {
        int c=1;
```

```
                m_GraphTextFile.Open(pathName, CStdioFile::modeRead);
                m_GraphTextFile.SeekToBegin();
                while(m_FileLine<=497)
                {
                        if(m_GraphTextFile.ReadString(xstr1)!=NULL)
m_FileLine++;

                }
                while(c<m_FileLine)
                {
                        if(m_GraphTextFile.ReadString(xstr1)!=NULL)
                                c++;
                }
                if(m_GraphTextFile.ReadString(xstr1)!=NULL)
                {
                        int drawCheck = GetUnipenData(xstr1);
                        if(drawCheck==1)
                        {
                                AdjustUnipenDataList(&m_graphPointList);
                                UINT xCurrentPoint, yCurrentPoint;
                                POSITION aPos =
m_graphPointList.GetHeadPosition();
                                while(aPos)
                                {
                                        FloatPoint =
m_graphPointList.GetNext(aPos);
                                        xCurrentPoint =
(UINT)FloatPoint.xFloat + 30;
                                        yCurrentPoint =
(UINT)FloatPoint.yFloat + 30;
                                        if(xCurrentPoint<=500 || yCurrentPoint
<=600)
                                                DrawDot(xCurrentPoint, yCurrentPoint);
                                }
                        }
                        m_FileLine++;
                }
                m_GraphTextFile.Close();
        }
        else
        {
                m_GraphTextFile.Open(pathName, CFile::modeRead);
                m_GraphTextFile.SeekToBegin();
                while(m_GraphTextFile.ReadString(xstr1)!=NULL)
                {
                        FloatPoint.xFloat = atof(xstr1);
                        m_GraphTextFile.ReadString(xstr1);
                        FloatPoint.yFloat = -atof(xstr1);
                        m_graphPointList.AddTail(FloatPoint);
                }

                UINT xCurrentPoint, yCurrentPoint;
                POSITION aPos = m_graphPointList.GetHeadPosition();

                while(aPos)
                {
                        FloatPoint = m_graphPointList.GetNext(aPos);
```

```
                    xCurrentPoint = (UINT)FloatPoint.xFloat + 30;
                    yCurrentPoint = (UINT)FloatPoint.yFloat + 30;
                    if(xCurrentPoint<=500 || yCurrentPoint <=600)
                        DrawDot(xCurrentPoint, yCurrentPoint);
            }
            m_GraphTextFile.Close();
        }
}

void CGraph::AdjustUnipenDataList(CList<CFloatPoint, const
CFloatPoint&> *m_graphPointList)
{
    double maxy=-10000000, miny=100000, maxx = -1000000;//, xr,
yr, dis;
    CFloatPoint FloatPoint;
    POSITION aPos = m_graphPointList->GetHeadPosition();
POSITION a;
    while(aPos)
    {
        FloatPoint = m_graphPointList->GetNext(aPos);
        if(FloatPoint.yFloat>maxy) maxy = FloatPoint.yFloat;
        if(FloatPoint.yFloat<miny) miny = FloatPoint.yFloat;
        if(FloatPoint.xFloat>maxx) maxx = FloatPoint.xFloat;
    }
    aPos = m_graphPointList->GetHeadPosition();
    while(aPos)
    {
        a = aPos;
        FloatPoint = m_graphPointList->GetNext(aPos);
        FloatPoint.yFloat*=-1;//+=fabs(miny);
        m_graphPointList->SetAt(a, FloatPoint);
    }


}

int CGraph::GetUnipenData(CString xstr1)
{
    int i=0; char *stops; //tt for boolean
    CString x, y; CFloatPoint FloatPoint;
    if(xstr1.GetLength()<=20) return 0;
    while(i<xstr1.GetLength())
    {
        if(xstr1.GetAt(i)=='S')    { i++; continue;}
        if(xstr1.GetAt(i)=='X')
        {
            i++;
            while(xstr1.GetAt(i)!='Y')
            {
                x+=xstr1.GetAt(i); i++;
            }
            FloatPoint.xFloat = strtod(x, &stops); x.Empty();
i++;

            while(xstr1.GetAt(i)!='X')
            {
```

```
                    if(xstr1.GetAt(i)=='S') break;
                    else if(xstr1.GetAt(i)==';') break;
                    y+=xstr1.GetAt(i); i++;
                }
                FloatPoint.yFloat = strtod(y, &stops); y.Empty();
                m_graphPointList.AddTail(FloatPoint); continue;
            }
            if(xstr1.GetAt(i)==';') break;
            i++;
        }
        return 1;
}

void CGraph::PlotPoints(UINT x, UINT y, UINT prevx, UINT prevy)
{
        DrawDot(x,y);

            return;
}


void CGraph::DrawDot(UINT X, UINT Y)
{
        char b[20];
        if (!m_pWnd)
        {
            return;
        }

        CPen pen;
        pen.CreatePen(PS_SOLID,3,m_crGraphPenColor);
        CDC *pdc=m_pWnd->GetDC();
        CPen *poldpen=pdc->SelectObject(&pen);
        _itoa_s(m_FileLine, b, 20, 10); pdc->TextOutA(300, 300, b);
        pdc->MoveTo(X,Y);
        pdc->LineTo(X,Y);

        pdc->SelectObject(poldpen);
        m_pWnd->ReleaseDC(pdc);

}
void CGraph::DrawConnectLine(UINT FromX, UINT FromY, UINT ToX,
UINT ToY)
{
        //draws a connecting line between to pixels
        //using the graphpen color

        if(!m_pWnd)
        {
            return;
        }
        //for the PLOTXY graphtype the user is not

        CPen pen, *poldpen;
        pen.CreatePen(PS_SOLID,1,m_crGraphPenColor);
        CDC *pdc=m_pWnd->GetDC();
        poldpen=pdc->SelectObject(&pen);
```

```cpp
        pdc->MoveTo(FromX,FromY);
        pdc->LineTo(ToX,ToY);

        pdc->SelectObject(poldpen);

        m_pWnd->ReleaseDC(pdc);
}

double CGraph::ConstrainY(double y)
{
        if ( (y < m_dYAxisMax) && (y > m_dYAxisMin))
        {
                return y;
        }

        else if (y <= m_dYAxisMin)
        {
                return m_dYAxisMin;
        }
        else if (y >=m_dYAxisMax)
        {
                return m_dYAxisMax;
        }
        return y; //should never get here???
}

COLORREF CGraph::GetMultiPlotPenColor(UINT PenNumber)
{
        //keep the pen within range
        PenNumber=PenNumber%G_NUM_MULTIPLOT_COLORS;
        switch(PenNumber)
        {
        case 0:
                return G_MULTIPLOT_COLOR_ONE;
                break;
        case 1:
                return G_MULTIPLOT_COLOR_TWO;
                break;
        case 2:
                return G_MULTIPLOT_COLOR_THREE;
                break;
        case 3:
                return G_MULTIPLOT_COLOR_FOUR;
                break;
        case 4:
                return G_MULTIPLOT_COLOR_FIVE;
                break;
        case 5:
                return G_MULTIPLOT_COLOR_SIX;
                break;
        case 6:
                return G_MULTIPLOT_COLOR_SEVEN;
                break;
        case 7:
```

```
            return G_MULTIPLOT_COLOR_EIGHT;
            break;
    default:
            return G_MULTIPLOT_COLOR_ONE;
    }

}
```

///Graphdialog

```cpp
// GraphDialog.cpp : implementation file
//

#include "stdafx.h"
#include "HWRAnuj.h"
#include "Graph.h"
#include "String.h"
#include "GraphDialog.h"

#ifdef _DEBUG
#define new DEBUG_NEW
#undef THIS_FILE
static char THIS_FILE[] = __FILE__;
#endif


// CGraphDialog dialog


CGraphDialog::CGraphDialog(CWnd* pParent /*=NULL*/)
    : CDialog(CGraphDialog::IDD, pParent)
{
    m_hIcon = AfxGetApp()->LoadIcon(IDR_MAINFRAME);

    m_pGraph=NULL;
    m_Scale = -1;
}


void CGraphDialog::DoDataExchange(CDataExchange* pDX)
{
    CDialog::DoDataExchange(pDX);
}


BEGIN_MESSAGE_MAP(CGraphDialog, CDialog)
    ON_BN_CLICKED(IDC_ORIGINAL, OnOriginal)
    ON_BN_CLICKED(IDC_SIZECENTER, OnSizeCenter)
    ON_BN_CLICKED(IDC_INTERPOLATION, OnInterpolation)
    ON_BN_CLICKED(IDC_SLANTCORRECTION, OnSlantCorrection)
    ON_BN_CLICKED(IDC_SMOOTH, OnSmooth)
    ON_BN_CLICKED(IDC_RESAMPLING, OnResampling)
    END_MESSAGE_MAP()


// CGraphDialog message handlers

void CGraphDialog::ToCallOnGraph()
{
    OnGraph();
}

void CGraphDialog::OnGraph()
{
```

```cpp
        if(m_pPlotItems !=NULL)
        {
            delete []m_pPlotItems;
            m_pPlotItems=NULL;
        }
        if(m_lpfs !=NULL)
        {
            m_pGraph->ClearFunction();
            delete m_lpfs;
        }
        m_pGraph->m_GraphType=0;
        m_pGraph->SetGraphSizePos(0,0,600,250);
        m_lpfs =new G_FUNCTIONSTRUCT;
        memset(m_lpfs,0,sizeof(G_FUNCTIONSTRUCT));

        m_lpfs->FuncType=G_GRAPH;
        m_lpfs->szGraphTitle="Normalized Character";
        m_lpfs->szXLegend="x-axis";
        m_lpfs->szYLegend="y-axis";
        m_lpfs->xMax=500;
        m_lpfs->xMin=0;
        m_lpfs->yMax=0;
        m_lpfs->yMin=-300;
        m_lpfs->Const_1=10;//the 'a' constant goes here
        m_lpfs->ChartType=G_DOTCHART;

        m_pGraph->DoFunction(m_lpfs);

}

void CGraphDialog::AddToListBox()
{
    m_PointRecordFileXls.Open("C:\\hwr\\POINTS-
TEXTSMOOTHING.xls",
            CFile::modeRead);
    m_PointRecordFileXls.SeekToBegin();
    pListBox->AddString("X          |         Y");
    while(m_PointRecordFileXls.ReadString(m_ListDataStr)!=NULL)
            pListBox->AddString(m_ListDataStr);
    pListBox->SetCurSel(m_Scale-1);
    m_PointRecordFileXls.Close();
}

BOOL CGraphDialog::OnInitDialog()
{
    CDialog::OnInitDialog();

    SetIcon(m_hIcon, TRUE),                 // Set big icon
    SetIcon(m_hIcon, FALSE);        // Set small icon

    m_pGraph=new CGraph(this,0,0,0,0,G_WHITESCHEME);
    m_lpfs=NULL;
    m_pPlotItems=NULL;

//    pListBox =
static_cast<CListBox*>(GetDlgItem(IDC_GRAPHDATALIST));
//    AddToListBox();
```

```
            return TRUE;
}

void CGraphDialog::OnSysCommand(UINT nID, LPARAM lParam)
{
        CDialog::OnSysCommand(nID, lParam);

}

void CGraphDialog::OnPaint()
{
        CPaintDC dc(this);

        if (IsIconic())
        {

                SendMessage(WM_ICONERASEBKGND, (WPARAM)
dc.GetSafeHdc(), 0);

                // Center icon in client rectangle
                int cxIcon = GetSystemMetrics(SM_CXICON);
                int cyIcon = GetSystemMetrics(SM_CYICON);
                CRect rect;
                GetClientRect(&rect);
                int x = (rect.Width() - cxIcon + 1) / 2;
                int y = (rect.Height() - cyIcon + 1) / 2;

                // Draw the icon
                dc.DrawIcon(x, y, m_hIcon);
        }
        else
        {
                CDialog::OnPaint();
                m_pGraph->PaintGraph();
        }
}

void CGraphDialog::OnDestroy()
{
        CDialog::OnDestroy();

        // TODO: Add your message handler code here
        if (m_pGraph)
        {
                delete m_pGraph;
        }

        if(m_lpfs)
        {
                delete m_lpfs;
        }
        if(m_pPlotItems !=NULL)
        {
                delete m_pPlotItems;
        }
}
```

```cpp
void CGraphDialog::OnNextCharacter()
{
    if(m_pPlotItems !=NULL)
    {
        delete []m_pPlotItems;
        m_pPlotItems=NULL;
    }
    if(m_lpfs !=NULL)
    {
        m_pGraph->ClearFunction();
        delete m_lpfs;
    }
    m_pGraph->m_GraphType=6;
    m_pGraph->SetGraphSizePos(0,0,600,250);
    m_lpfs =new G_FUNCTIONSTRUCT;
    memset(m_lpfs,0,sizeof(G_FUNCTIONSTRUCT));

    m_lpfs->FuncType=G_GRAPH;
    m_lpfs->szGraphTitle="Character from UNIPEN Files...";
    m_lpfs->szXLegend="x-axis";
    m_lpfs->szYLegend="y-axis";
    m_lpfs->xMax=500;
    m_lpfs->xMin=0;
    m_lpfs->yMax=0;
    m_lpfs->yMin=-300;
    m_lpfs->Const_1=10;//the 'a' constant goes here
    m_lpfs->ChartType=G_DOTCHART;
    m_pGraph->DoFunction(m_lpfs);

}

void CGraphDialog::OnCloseExit()
{
    if(m_pPlotItems !=NULL)
    {
        delete []m_pPlotItems;
        m_pPlotItems=NULL;
    }
    if(m_lpfs !=NULL)
    {
        m_pGraph->ClearFunction();
        delete m_lpfs;
    }
    exit(0);
}

void CGraphDialog::OnOriginal()
{
    if(m_pPlotItems !=NULL)
    {
        delete []m_pPlotItems;
        m_pPlotItems=NULL;
    }
    if(m_lpfs !=NULL)
    {
        m_pGraph->ClearFunction();
        delete m_lpfs;
```

```
        }
        m_pGraph->m_GraphType=1;
        m_pGraph->SetGraphSizePos(0,0,600,250);
        m_lpfs =new G_FUNCTIONSTRUCT;
        memset(m_lpfs,0,sizeof(G_FUNCTIONSTRUCT));

        //function is: a*sin(x)  //from x=xMin to x=xMax radians
        m_lpfs->FuncType=G_GRAPH;
        m_lpfs->szGraphTitle="Original Text";
        m_lpfs->szXLegend="x-axis";
        m_lpfs->szYLegend="y-axis";
        m_lpfs->xMax=500;
        m_lpfs->xMin=0;
        m_lpfs->yMax=0;
        m_lpfs->yMin=-300;
        m_lpfs->Const_1=10;//the 'a' constant goes here
        m_lpfs->ChartType=G_DOTCHART;
        m_pGraph->DoFunction(m_lpfs);

}

void CGraphDialog::OnSizeCenter()
{
        if(m_pPlotItems !=NULL)
        {
             delete []m_pPlotItems;
             m_pPlotItems=NULL;
        }
        if(m_lpfs !=NULL)
        {
             m_pGraph->ClearFunction();
             delete m_lpfs;
        }

        m_pGraph->m_GraphType=2;
        m_pGraph->SetGraphSizePos(0,0,600,250);
        m_lpfs =new G_FUNCTIONSTRUCT;
        memset(m_lpfs,0,sizeof(G_FUNCTIONSTRUCT));

        //function is: a*sin(x)  //from x=xMin to x=xMax radians
        m_lpfs->FuncType=G_GRAPH;
        m_lpfs->szGraphTitle="Size Normalization and Centering";
        m_lpfs->szXLegend="x-axis";
        m_lpfs->szYLegend="y-axis";
        m_lpfs->xMax=500;
        m_lpfs->xMin=0;
        m_lpfs->yMax=0;
        m_lpfs->yMin=-300;
        m_lpfs->Const_1=10;//the 'a' constant goes here
        m_lpfs->ChartType=G_DOTCHART;

        m_pGraph->DoFunction(m_lpfs);
}

void CGraphDialog::OnInterpolation()
{
        if(m_pPlotItems !=NULL)
```

```
        {
            delete []m_pPlotItems;
            m_pPlotItems=NULL;
        }
        if(m_lpfs !=NULL)
        {
            m_pGraph->ClearFunction();
            delete m_lpfs;
        }

        m_pGraph->m_GraphType=3;
        m_pGraph->SetGraphSizePos(0,0,600,250);
        m_lpfs =new G_FUNCTIONSTRUCT;
        memset(m_lpfs,0,sizeof(G_FUNCTIONSTRUCT));

        //function is: a*sin(x) //from x=xMin to x=xMax radians
        m_lpfs->FuncType=G_GRAPH;
        m_lpfs->szGraphTitle="Interpolating Missing Points";
        m_lpfs->szXLegend="x-axis";
        m_lpfs->szYLegend="y-axis";
        m_lpfs->xMax=500;
        m_lpfs->xMin=0;
        m_lpfs->yMax=0;
        m_lpfs->yMin=-300;
        m_lpfs->Const_1=10;//the 'a' constant goes here
        m_lpfs->ChartType=G_DOTCHART;

        m_pGraph->DoFunction(m_lpfs);
}

void CGraphDialog::OnSmooth()
{
        if(m_pPlotItems !=NULL)
        {
            delete []m_pPlotItems;
            m_pPlotItems=NULL;
        }
        if(m_lpfs !=NULL)
        {
            m_pGraph->ClearFunction();
            delete m_lpfs;
        }
        m_pGraph->m_GraphType=4;
        m_pGraph->SetGraphSizePos(0,0,600,250);
        m_lpfs =new G_FUNCTIONSTRUCT;
        memset(m_lpfs,0,sizeof(G_FUNCTIONSTRUCT));

        //function is: a*sin(x) //from x=xMin to x=xMax radians
        m_lpfs->FuncType=G_GRAPH;
        m_lpfs->szGraphTitle="Smoothing and Slant Correction";
        m_lpfs->szXLegend="x-axis";
        m_lpfs->szYLegend="y-axis";
        m_lpfs->xMax=500;
        m_lpfs->xMin=0;
        m_lpfs->yMax=0;
        m_lpfs->yMin=-300;
        m_lpfs->Const_1=10;//the 'a' constant goes here
```

```
        m_lpfs->ChartType=G_DOTCHART;

        m_pGraph->DoFunction(m_lpfs);
}

void CGraphDialog::OnSlantCorrection()
{
        if(m_pPlotItems !=NULL)
        {
                delete []m_pPlotItems;
                m_pPlotItems=NULL;
        }
        if(m_lpfs !=NULL)
        {
                m_pGraph->ClearFunction();
                delete m_lpfs;
        }

        m_pGraph->m_GraphType=5;
        m_pGraph->SetGraphSizePos(0,0,600,250);
        m_lpfs =new G_FUNCTIONSTRUCT;
        memset(m_lpfs,0,sizeof(G_FUNCTIONSTRUCT));

        //function is: a*sin(x)  //from x=xMin to x=xMax radians
        m_lpfs->FuncType=G_GRAPH;
        m_lpfs->szGraphTitle="Slant Correction of Input Text";
        m_lpfs->szXLegend="x-axis";
        m_lpfs->szYLegend="y-axis";
        m_lpfs->xMax=500;
        m_lpfs->xMin=0;
        m_lpfs->yMax=0;
        m_lpfs->yMin=-300;
        m_lpfs->Const_1=10;//the 'a' constant goes here
        m_lpfs->ChartType=G_DOTCHART;

        m_pGraph->DoFunction(m_lpfs);
}

void CGraphDialog::OnResampling()
{
        if(m_pPlotItems !=NULL)
        {
                delete []m_pPlotItems;
                m_pPlotItems=NULL;
        }
        if(m_lpfs !=NULL)
        {
                m_pGraph->ClearFunction();
                delete m_lpfs;
        }
        m_pGraph->m_GraphType=7;
        m_pGraph->SetGraphSizePos(0,0,600,250);
        m_lpfs =new G_FUNCTIONSTRUCT;
        memset(m_lpfs,0,sizeof(G_FUNCTIONSTRUCT));

        m_lpfs->FuncType=G_GRAPH;
        m_lpfs->szGraphTitle="Resampling of Points";
```

```
        m_lpfs->szXLegend="x-axis";
        m_lpfs->szYLegend="y-axis";
        m_lpfs->xMax=500;
        m_lpfs->xMin=0;
        m_lpfs->yMax=0;
        m_lpfs->yMin=-300;
        m_lpfs->Const_1=10;//the 'a' constant goes here
        m_lpfs->ChartType=G_DOTCHART;

        m_pGraph->DoFunction(m_lpfs);
}


void CGraphDialog::OnClearGraph()
{
        m_pGraph->ClearFunction();
}

void CGraphDialog::OnFEResults()
{
        CString pszParseName;
        pszParseName="c:\\hwr\\Features.txt";
        SHELLEXECUTEINFO ShExecInfo;

        ShExecInfo.cbSize = sizeof(SHELLEXECUTEINFO);
    ShExecInfo.fMask = NULL;
    ShExecInfo.hwnd = NULL;
    ShExecInfo.lpVerb = NULL;
    ShExecInfo.lpFile = pszParseName;
    ShExecInfo.lpParameters = NULL;
    ShExecInfo.lpDirectory = NULL;
    ShExecInfo.nShow = SW_MAXIMIZE;
    ShExecInfo.hInstApp = NULL;

        ShellExecuteEx(&ShExecInfo);
}
```

CHAPTER 5

MISCELLANEOUS FILES FOR INTERFACE

2.3 Other Necessary Development Class Files

```
#include "stdafx.h"
#include "math.h"
#include "String.h"
#include "Stdlib.h"
#include "OurConstants.h"
#include "DataFile.h"
#include "Elements.h"

IMPLEMENT_SERIAL(CElement, CObject, VERSION_NUMBER)
IMPLEMENT_SERIAL(CLine, CElement, VERSION_NUMBER)
IMPLEMENT_SERIAL(CRectangle, CElement, VERSION_NUMBER)
IMPLEMENT_SERIAL(CCircle,CElement, VERSION_NUMBER)
IMPLEMENT_SERIAL(CCurve,CElement, VERSION_NUMBER)
IMPLEMENT_SERIAL(CEllipse,CElement, VERSION_NUMBER)
IMPLEMENT_SERIAL(CText,CElement, VERSION_NUMBER)

void CElement::Serialize(CArchive& ar)
{
    CObject::Serialize(ar);

    if(ar.IsStoring())
    {
        ar<<m_Color<<m_EnclosingRect<<m_Pen;
    }
    else
    {
        ar>>m_Color>>m_EnclosingRect>>m_Pen;
    }
}

CLine :: CLine(const CPoint& Start, const CPoint& End,
               const COLORREF& Color, int PenStyle, const int& PenWidth)
{
    m_StartPoint=Start;
    m_EndPoint=End;
    m_Color=Color;
    m_PenStyle=PenStyle;
    m_Pen=PenWidth;

    m_EnclosingRect=CRect(Start,End);
    m_EnclosingRect.NormalizeRect();
```

```
}

void CLine::Draw(CDC *pDC, const CElement* pElement) const
{
      CPen aPen;
      COLORREF aColor = m_Color;
      if(this == pElement)
            aColor = SELECT_COLOR;
      if(!aPen.CreatePen(m_PenStyle,m_Pen,aColor))
      {
            AfxMessageBox("Pen creation failed drawing a line",MB_OK);
            AfxAbort();
      }

      CPen* pOldPen = pDC->SelectObject(&aPen);
      pDC->MoveTo(m_StartPoint);
      pDC->LineTo(m_EndPoint);
      pDC->SelectObject(pOldPen);
}

void CLine::Move(const CSize& aSize)
{
      m_StartPoint += aSize;
      m_EndPoint += aSize;
      m_EnclosingRect += aSize;
}

void CLine::Serialize(CArchive& ar)
{
      CElement::Serialize(ar);

      if(ar.IsStoring())
      {
            ar<<m_StartPoint<<m_EndPoint;
      }
      else
      {
            ar>>m_StartPoint>>m_EndPoint;
      }
}

CRect CElement :: GetBoundRect() const
{
      CRect BoundingRect;
      BoundingRect = m_EnclosingRect;

      int Offset=m_Pen == 0? 1: m_Pen;
      BoundingRect.InflateRect(Offset,Offset);

      return BoundingRect;

}

CRectangle::CRectangle(const CPoint& Start, const CPoint& End,
                         const COLORREF& Color, int PenStyle, const int& PenWidth)
```

```cpp
{
    m_Color=Color;
    m_Pen=PenWidth;
    m_PenStyle=PenStyle;

    m_EnclosingRect=CRect(Start,End);
    m_EnclosingRect.NormalizeRect();
}

void CRectangle::Draw(CDC *pDC, const CElement* pElement) const
{
    CPen aPen;
    COLORREF aColor = m_Color;
    if(this == pElement)
        aColor = SELECT_COLOR;
    if(!aPen.CreatePen(m_PenStyle,m_Pen,aColor))
    {
        AfxMessageBox("Pen creation failed drawing a Rectangle",MB_OK);
        AfxAbort();
    }

    CPen* pOldPen = pDC->SelectObject(&aPen);
    CBrush* pOldBrush = static_cast<CBrush*>(pDC->SelectStockObject(NULL_BRUSH));

    pDC->Rectangle(m_EnclosingRect);

    pDC->SelectObject(pOldBrush);
    pDC->SelectObject(pOldPen);
}

void CRectangle::Move(const CSize& aSize)
{
    m_EnclosingRect += aSize;
}

void CRectangle::Serialize(CArchive& ar)
{
    CElement::Serialize(ar);
}

CCircle::CCircle(const CPoint& Start, const CPoint& End,
                 const COLORREF& Color, int PenStyle, const int& PenWidth)
{
    long radius=static_cast<long>(sqrt(static_cast<double>(
        (End.x-Start.x)*(End.x-Start.x)+(End.y-Start.y)*(End.y-Start.y))));
    m_EnclosingRect=CRect(Start.x-radius, Start.y-radius,
        Start.x+radius,Start.y+radius);
    m_Color=Color;
    m_Pen=PenWidth;
    m_PenStyle=PenStyle;
}

void CCircle::Draw(CDC *pDC, const CElement* pElement) const
```

```
{
    CPen aPen;
    COLORREF aColor = m_Color;
    if(this == pElement)
        aColor = SELECT_COLOR;
    if(!aPen.CreatePen(m_PenStyle,m_Pen,aColor))
    {
        AfxMessageBox("Pen creation failed drawing a
Circle",MB_OK);
        AfxAbort();
    }

    CPen* pOldPen = pDC->SelectObject(&aPen);
    CBrush* pOldBrush = static_cast<CBrush*>(pDC-
>SelectStockObject(NULL_BRUSH));

    pDC->Ellipse(m_EnclosingRect);

    pDC->SelectObject(pOldBrush);
    pDC->SelectObject(pOldPen);
}
void CCircle::Move(const CSize& aSize)
{
    m_EnclosingRect += aSize;
}

void CCircle::Serialize(CArchive& ar)
{
    CElement::Serialize(ar);
}

CCurve::CCurve()
{

}

CCurve::CCurve(const CPoint& FirstPoint,const CPoint&
SecondPoint,
                const COLORREF& Color, int PenStyle, const
int& PenWidth)
{

    m_PointList.AddTail(FirstPoint);
    m_PointList.AddTail(SecondPoint);

    m_Color=Color;
    m_Pen=PenWidth;
    m_PenStyle=SOLID;

    m_EnclosingRect=CRect(FirstPoint, SecondPoint);
    m_EnclosingRect.NormalizeRect();

}

CCurve::~CCurve()
{
```

```
}

void CCurve::AddSegment(const CPoint& Point)
{
    m_PointList.AddTail(Point) ;
    m_EnclosingRect=CRect(min(Point.x,m_EnclosingRect.left),

    min(Point.y,m_EnclosingRect.top),

    max(Point.x,m_EnclosingRect.right),

    max(Point.y,m_EnclosingRect.bottom));
}

void CCurve::Draw(CDC* pDC, const CElement* pElement) const
{
    CPen aPen;
    COLORREF aColor = m_Color;

    if(this == pElement)
        aColor = SELECT_COLOR;
    if(!aPen.CreatePen(m_PenStyle,m_Pen,aColor))
    {
        AfxMessageBox("Pen creation failed drawing a Curve",MB_OK);
        AfxAbort();
    }

    CPen* pOldPen = pDC->SelectObject(&aPen);

    POSITION aPosition=m_PointList.GetHeadPosition();

    if(aPosition)
        pDC->MoveTo(m_PointList.GetNext(aPosition));

    while(aPosition)
    {
        pDC->LineTo(m_PointList.GetNext(aPosition));
    }
    pDC->SelectObject(pOldPen);

}

void CCurve::temp()
{
    m_PointList.RemoveAll();
}

void CCurve ::Move(const CSize& aSize)
{
    m_EnclosingRect += aSize;
    POSITION aPosition = m_PointList.GetHeadPosition();
    while(aPosition)
        m_PointList.GetNext(aPosition) += aSize;
}
```

```
void CCurve::Serialize(CArchive& ar)
{
    CElement::Serialize(ar);
    m_PointList.Serialize(ar);
}

CEllipse::CEllipse(const CPoint& Start, const CPoint& End,
                   const COLORREF& Color, int PenStyle,
const int& PenWidth)
{
    m_Color=Color;
    m_Pen=PenWidth;
    m_PenStyle=PenStyle;
    m_EnclosingRect=CRect(Start,End);
    m_EnclosingRect.NormalizeRect();
}

void CEllipse::Draw(CDC *pDC, const CElement* pElement) const
{
    CPen aPen;
    COLORREF aColor = m_Color;
    if(this == pElement)
         aColor = SELECT_COLOR;
    if(!aPen.CreatePen(m_PenStyle,m_Pen,aColor))
    {
         AfxMessageBox("Pen creation failed drawing a
Ellipse",MB_OK);
         AfxAbort();
    }

    CPen* pOldPen = pDC->SelectObject(&aPen);
    CBrush* pOldBrush = static_cast<CBrush*>(pDC-
>SelectStockObject(NULL_BRUSH));

    pDC->Ellipse(m_EnclosingRect);

    pDC->SelectObject(pOldBrush);
    pDC->SelectObject(pOldPen);
}
void CEllipse::Move(const CSize& aSize)
{
    m_EnclosingRect += aSize;
}

void CEllipse::Serialize(CArchive& ar)
{
    CElement::Serialize(ar);
}

CText::CText(const CPoint& Start, const CPoint& End,
         const CString& String, const COLORREF& Color,
         int PenStyle, const int& PenWidth)
{
    m_Pen = 1;
    m_Color = Color;
    m_String = String;
```

```
      m_StartPoint = Start;
      m_PenStyle = PenStyle;
      m_Pen = PenWidth;

      m_EnclosingRect = CRect(Start, End);
      m_EnclosingRect.NormalizeRect();
}

void CText::Draw(CDC* pDC, const CElement* pElement) const
{
      COLORREF Color(m_Color);
      if(this == pElement)
            Color = SELECT_COLOR;

      pDC->SetTextColor(Color);
      pDC->TextOut(m_StartPoint.x, m_StartPoint.y, m_String);
}

void CText::Move(const CSize& aSize)
{
      m_StartPoint += aSize;
      m_EnclosingRect += aSize;
}

void CText::Serialize(CArchive& ar)
{
      CElement::Serialize(ar);

      if(ar.IsStoring())
      {
            ar<<m_StartPoint<<m_String;
      }
      else
      {
            ar>>m_StartPoint>>m_String;
      }
}
```

```cpp
// MainFrm.cpp : implementation of the CMainFrame class
//

#include "stdafx.h"
#include "HWRAnuj.h"

#include "MainFrm.h"

#ifdef _DEBUG
#define new DEBUG_NEW
#undef THIS_FILE
static char THIS_FILE[] = __FILE__;
#endif


// CMainFrame

IMPLEMENT_DYNAMIC(CMainFrame, CMDIFrameWnd)

BEGIN_MESSAGE_MAP(CMainFrame, CMDIFrameWnd)
    //{{AFX_MSG_MAP(CMainFrame)
    ON_WM_CREATE()
    //}}AFX_MSG_MAP
END_MESSAGE_MAP()

static UINT indicators[] =
{
    ID_SEPARATOR,           // status line indicator
    ID_INDICATOR_CAPS,
    ID_INDICATOR_NUM,
    ID_INDICATOR_SCRL,
};


// CMainFrame construction/destruction

CMainFrame::CMainFrame()
{
    // TODO: add member initialization code here

}

CMainFrame::~CMainFrame()
{

}

int CMainFrame::OnCreate(LPCREATESTRUCT lpCreateStruct)
{
    if (CMDIFrameWnd::OnCreate(lpCreateStruct) == -1)
        return -1;

    if (!m_wndToolBar.CreateEx(this, TBSTYLE_FLAT, WS_CHILD | WS_VISIBLE | CBRS_TOP
        | CBRS_GRIPPER | CBRS_TOOLTIPS | CBRS_FLYBY | CBRS_SIZE_DYNAMIC) ||
        !m_wndToolBar.LoadToolBar(IDR_MAINFRAME))
```

```
    {
        TRACE0("Failed to create toolbar\n");
        return -1;      // fail to create
    }

    if (!m_wndStatusBar.Create(this) ||
        !m_wndStatusBar.SetIndicators(indicators,
          sizeof(indicators)/sizeof(UINT)))
    {
        TRACE0("Failed to create status bar\n");
        return -1;      // fail to create
    }

    m_wndToolBar.EnableDocking(CBRS_ALIGN_ANY);
    EnableDocking(CBRS_ALIGN_ANY);
    DockControlBar(&m_wndToolBar);

    return 0;
}

BOOL CMainFrame::PreCreateWindow(CREATESTRUCT& cs)
{

    if( !CMDIFrameWnd::PreCreateWindow(cs) )
        return FALSE;

    return TRUE;
}


// CMainFrame diagnostics

#ifdef _DEBUG
void CMainFrame::AssertValid() const
{
    CMDIFrameWnd::AssertValid();
}

void CMainFrame::Dump(CDumpContext& dc) const
{
    CMDIFrameWnd::Dump(dc);
}

void CMainFrame::SetPaneText(int Pane, LPCTSTR Text)
{
    m_wndStatusBar.SetPaneText(Pane, Text);
}
#endif //_DEBUG
```

```cpp
#include "stdafx.h"
#include "Elements.h"
#include "HWRAnuj.h"
#include "ChildFrm.h"
///included below for Splitter window
/*
#include "ScaleDialog.h"
#include "TextDialog.h"
#include "ToolsDialog.h"
#include "DataFile.h"
#include "Preprocessing.h"
#include "Math.h"
#include "Normalize.h"
#include "GraphDialog.h"
#include "Graph.h"
#include "HWRAnuj.h"
#include "String.h"
#include "Stdlib.h"
#include "Elements.h"
#include "RecognitionDialog.h"
#include "HWRAnujDoc.h"
#include "HWRAnujView.h"
*/

#ifdef _DEBUG
#define new DEBUG_NEW
#undef THIS_FILE
static char THIS_FILE[] = __FILE__;
#endif


// CChildFrame

IMPLEMENT_DYNCREATE(CChildFrame, CMDIChildWnd)

BEGIN_MESSAGE_MAP(CChildFrame, CMDIChildWnd)
    //{{AFX_MSG_MAP(CChildFrame)
    ON_WM_CREATE()
    //}}AFX_MSG_MAP
END_MESSAGE_MAP()


// CChildFrame construction/destruction

CChildFrame::CChildFrame()
{
    // TODO: add member initialization code here

}

CChildFrame::~CChildFrame()
{
}

BOOL CChildFrame::PreCreateWindow(CREATESTRUCT& cs)
{
    // TODO: Modify the Window class or styles here by modifying
```

```cpp
        //   the CREATESTRUCT cs

    if( !CMDIChildWnd::PreCreateWindow(cs) )
            return FALSE;

    return TRUE;
}

// CChildFrame diagnostics

#ifdef _DEBUG
void CChildFrame::AssertValid() const
{
    CMDIChildWnd::AssertValid();
}

void CChildFrame::Dump(CDumpContext& dc) const
{
    CMDIChildWnd::Dump(dc);
}

#endif //_DEBUG


// CChildFrame message handlers

///included below for Splitter window

/*
BOOL CChildFrame::OnCreateClient(LPCREATESTRUCT , CCreateContext* pContext)
{
    // create splitter window
    if (!m_wndSplitter.CreateStatic(this, 1, 2))
            return FALSE;

    if (!m_wndSplitter.CreateView(0, 0,
RUNTIME_CLASS(CHWRAnujView), CSize(500, 100), pContext) ||
        !m_wndSplitter.CreateView(0, 1,
RUNTIME_CLASS(CHWRAnujView), CSize(100, 100), pContext))
    {
            m_wndSplitter.DestroyWindow();
            return FALSE;
    }
    return TRUE;
}
*/
int CChildFrame::OnCreate(LPCREATESTRUCT lpCreateStruct)
{
    if (CMDIChildWnd::OnCreate(lpCreateStruct) == -1)
            return -1;

    // TODO: Add your specialized creation code here
    ShowWindow(SW_MAXIMIZE); ///to show child window maximized

    m_StatusBar.Create(this);
    CRect textRect;
```

```
    CClientDC aDC(&m_StatusBar);
    aDC.SelectObject(m_StatusBar.GetFont());
    aDC.DrawText("WRAnuj - View Scale:99", -1, textRect,
DT_SINGLELINE|DT_CALCRECT);

    int width=textRect.Width();
    m_StatusBar.GetStatusBarCtrl().SetParts(1,&width);

    m_StatusBar.GetStatusBarCtrl().SetText("WRAnuj - View
Scale:1",0,0) ;

    return 0;
}
```

```cpp
// ToolsDialog.cpp : implementation file
//

#include "stdafx.h"
#include "HWRAnuj.h"
#include "Elements.h"
#include "DataFile.h"
#include "HWRAnujDoc.h"
#include "HWRAnujView.h"
#include "String.h"
#include "Stdlib.h"
#include "ToolsDialog.h"

#ifdef _DEBUG
#define new DEBUG_NEW
#undef THIS_FILE
static char THIS_FILE[] = __FILE__;
#endif


// CToolsDialog dialog


CToolsDialog::CToolsDialog(CWnd* pParent /*=NULL*/)
    : CDialog(CToolsDialog::IDD, pParent)
{
    //{{AFX_DATA_INIT(CToolsDialog)

        // NOTE: the ClassWizard will add member initialization here
    //}}AFX_DATA_INIT
}

void CToolsDialog::DoDataExchange(CDataExchange* pDX)
{
    CDialog::DoDataExchange(pDX);
    //{{AFX_DATA_MAP(CToolsDialog)

        // NOTE: the ClassWizard will add DDX and DDV calls here
    //}}AFX_DATA_MAP
}


BEGIN_MESSAGE_MAP(CToolsDialog, CDialog)
    //{{AFX_MSG_MAP(CToolsDialog)
    ON_BN_CLICKED(IDC_DATAFILE, OnDataFile)
    //}}AFX_MSG_MAP
END_MESSAGE_MAP()


BOOL CToolsDialog::OnInitDialog()
{
    CDialog::OnInitDialog();
    CButton* pButton = static_cast<CButton*>(GetDlgItem(IDC_DATAFILE));
```

```
        return TRUE;
}

// CToolsDialog message handlers

void CToolsDialog::OnDataFile()
{
        // TODO: Add your control notification handler code here
//      CDataFile dataFile;
//      dataFile.AddToDataFile();
}
```

```
//CTextDialog File
#include "stdafx.h"
#include "HWRAnuj.h"
#include "Resource.h"
#include "TextDialog.h"

#ifdef _DEBUG
#define new DEBUG_NEW
#undef THIS_FILE
static char THIS_FILE[] = __FILE__;
#endif


// CTextDialog dialog


CTextDialog::CTextDialog(CWnd* pParent /*=NULL*/)
    : CDialog(CTextDialog::IDD, pParent)
{
    //{{AFX_DATA_INIT(CTextDialog)
    m_TextString = _T("");
    //}}AFX_DATA_INIT
}


void CTextDialog::DoDataExchange(CDataExchange* pDX)
{
    CDialog::DoDataExchange(pDX);
    //{{AFX_DATA_MAP(CTextDialog)
    DDX_Text(pDX, IDC_EDITTEXT, m_TextString);
    DDV_MaxChars(pDX, m_TextString, 100);
    //}}AFX_DATA_MAP
}


BEGIN_MESSAGE_MAP(CTextDialog, CDialog)
    //{{AFX_MSG_MAP(CTextDialog)
        // NOTE: the ClassWizard will add message map macros here
    //}}AFX_MSG_MAP
END_MESSAGE_MAP()
```

```cpp
// ScaleDialog.cpp : implementation file
//

#include "stdafx.h"
#include "HWRAnuj.h"
#include "ScaleDialog.h"

#ifdef _DEBUG
#define new DEBUG_NEW
#undef THIS_FILE
static char THIS_FILE[] = __FILE__;
#endif


// CScaleDialog dialog


CScaleDialog::CScaleDialog(CWnd* pParent /*=NULL*/)
    : CDialog(CScaleDialog::IDD, pParent)
{
    //{{AFX_DATA_INIT(CScaleDialog)
    m_Scale = -1;
    //}}AFX_DATA_INIT
}


void CScaleDialog::DoDataExchange(CDataExchange* pDX)
{
    CDialog::DoDataExchange(pDX);
    //{{AFX_DATA_MAP(CScaleDialog)
    DDX_LBIndex(pDX, IDC_SCALELIST, m_Scale);
    //}}AFX_DATA_MAP
}


BEGIN_MESSAGE_MAP(CScaleDialog, CDialog)
    //{{AFX_MSG_MAP(CScaleDialog)
    //}}AFX_MSG_MAP
END_MESSAGE_MAP()


// CScaleDialog message handlers

BOOL CScaleDialog::OnInitDialog()
{
    CDialog::OnInitDialog();

    // TODO: Add extra initialisation here
    CListBox* pListBox =
static_cast<CListBox*>(GetDlgItem(IDC_SCALELIST));
    pListBox->AddString("Scale 1");
    pListBox->AddString("Scale 2");
    pListBox->AddString("Scale 3");
    pListBox->AddString("Scale 4");
    pListBox->AddString("Scale 5");
    pListBox->AddString("Scale 6");
    pListBox->AddString("Scale 7");
```

```
        pListBox->AddString("Scale 8");
        pListBox->SetCurSel(m_Scale - 1);

        return TRUE;  // return TRUE unless you set the focus to a control
                      // EXCEPTION: OCX Property Pages should return FALSE
}
```

```cpp
// PenDialog.cpp : implementation file
//

#include "stdafx.h"
#include "HWRAnuj.h"
#include "PenDialog.h"

#ifdef _DEBUG
#define new DEBUG_NEW
#undef THIS_FILE
static char THIS_FILE[] = __FILE__;
#endif


// CPenDialog dialog


CPenDialog::CPenDialog(CWnd* pParent /*=NULL*/)
    : CDialog(CPenDialog::IDD, pParent)
{
    //{{AFX_DATA_INIT(CPenDialog)
        // NOTE: the ClassWizard will add member initialization here
    //}}AFX_DATA_INIT
}


void CPenDialog::DoDataExchange(CDataExchange* pDX)
{
    CDialog::DoDataExchange(pDX);
    //{{AFX_DATA_MAP(CPenDialog)
        // NOTE: the ClassWizard will add DDX and DDV calls here
    //}}AFX_DATA_MAP
}


BEGIN_MESSAGE_MAP(CPenDialog, CDialog)
    //{{AFX_MSG_MAP(CPenDialog)
    ON_WM_CANCELMODE()
    ON_BN_CLICKED(IDC_PENWIDTH0, OnPenwidth0)
    ON_BN_CLICKED(IDC_PENWIDTH1, OnPenwidth1)
    ON_BN_CLICKED(IDC_PENWIDTH2, OnPenwidth2)
    ON_BN_CLICKED(IDC_PENWIDTH3, OnPenwidth3)
    ON_BN_CLICKED(IDC_PENWIDTH4, OnPenwidth4)
    ON_BN_CLICKED(IDC_PENWIDTH5, OnPenwidth5)
    //}}AFX_MSG_MAP
END_MESSAGE_MAP()


// CPenDialog message handlers

BOOL CPenDialog::OnInitDialog()
{
    CDialog::OnInitDialog();

    // TODO: Add extra initialization here
```

```cpp
        CDialog::OnInitDialog();
        switch(m_PenWidth)
        {
        case 1:
             CheckDlgButton(IDC_PENWIDTH1,1);
             break;
        case 2:
             CheckDlgButton(IDC_PENWIDTH2,1);
             break;
        case 3:
             CheckDlgButton(IDC_PENWIDTH3,1);
             break;
        case 4:
             CheckDlgButton(IDC_PENWIDTH4,1);
             break;
        case 5:
             CheckDlgButton(IDC_PENWIDTH5,1);
             break;
        default:
             CheckDlgButton(IDC_PENWIDTH0,1);
             break;

        }
     return TRUE;  // return TRUE unless you set the focus to a control
                   // EXCEPTION: OCX Property Pages should return FALSE
}

void CPenDialog::OnCancelMode()
{
     CDialog::OnCancelMode();

     // TODO: Add your message handler code here

}

void CPenDialog::OnPenwidth0()
{
     // TODO: Add your control notification handler code here
     m_PenWidth = 0;
}

void CPenDialog::OnPenwidth1()
{
     // TODO: Add your control notification handler code here
     m_PenWidth = 1;
}

void CPenDialog::OnPenwidth2()
{
     // TODO: Add your control notification handler code here
     m_PenWidth = 2;
}

void CPenDialog::OnPenwidth3()
{
```

```
        // TODO: Add your control notification handler code here
        m_PenWidth = 3;
}

void CPenDialog::OnPenwidth4()
{
        // TODO: Add your control notification handler code here
        m_PenWidth = 4;
}

void CPenDialog::OnPenwidth5()
{
        // TODO: Add your control notification handler code here
        m_PenWidth = 5;
}
```

```cpp
// InputWordDialog.cpp : implementation file
//

#include "stdafx.h"
#include "HWRAnuj.h"
#include "InputWordDialog.h"


// CInputWordDialog dialog
CString global_StrSelectedWord;
IMPLEMENT_DYNAMIC(CInputWordDialog, CDialog)

CInputWordDialog::CInputWordDialog(CWnd* pParent /*=NULL*/)
    : CDialog(CInputWordDialog::IDD, pParent)
{

}

CInputWordDialog::~CInputWordDialog()
{
}

void CInputWordDialog::DoDataExchange(CDataExchange* pDX)
{
    CDialog::DoDataExchange(pDX);
    //DDX_Text(pDX, IDC_WORD_LIST, m_Word);
    DDX_Text(pDX, IDC_SELECTED_WORD, m_Word);
    //DDV_MaxChars(pDX, m_Word, 100);
}


BEGIN_MESSAGE_MAP(CInputWordDialog, CDialog)

    ON_LBN_SELCHANGE(IDC_WORD_LIST,
&CInputWordDialog::OnLbnSelchangeWordList)
    ON_BN_CLICKED(IDC_ADD_WORD,
&CInputWordDialog::OnBnClickedAddWord)
END_MESSAGE_MAP()


// CInputWordDialog message handlers

BOOL CInputWordDialog::OnInitDialog()
{
    CDialog::OnInitDialog();

    CString Line, File; File="WordList.dat";
    pLB = new CListBox();
    pLB = reinterpret_cast<CListBox
*>(GetDlgItem(IDC_WORD_LIST));
    pFont = new CFont();
    pFont->CreateFont(18,0,0,0,700,0,0,0,
ANSI_CHARSET,OUT_DEFAULT_PRECIS, CLIP_DEFAULT_PRECIS,
DEFAULT_QUALITY, DEFAULT_PITCH|FF_DONTCARE, "GurbaniWebThick");
//"GurbaniHindiWeb");
    pLB->SetFont(pFont);
```

```
        if(!ObjF.Open(File, CStdioFile::modeCreate |
CStdioFile::modeNoTruncate | CStdioFile::modeReadWrite))      ///to
create file or check if already exists
        {}
        ObjF.SeekToBegin();
        while(ObjF.ReadString(Line)!=NULL)       pLB->AddString(Line);
        ObjF.Close();
        pFont2 = new CFont();
        pFont2->CreateFont(48,0,0,0,700,0,0,0,
ANSI_CHARSET,OUT_DEFAULT_PRECIS, CLIP_DEFAULT_PRECIS,
DEFAULT_QUALITY, DEFAULT_PITCH|FF_DONTCARE, "GurbaniWebThick");
//"GUrbaniHindiWeb");//
        pE = new CEdit();
        pE = reinterpret_cast<CEdit
*>(GetDlgItem(IDC_SELECTED_WORD));
        pE->SetFont(pFont2);
        int n = pLB->GetTextLen(pLB->GetCurSel()); pLB->GetText(0,
Line.GetBuffer(0));
        pE->SetWindowText(Line.GetBuffer(0));

        return TRUE;
}

void CInputWordDialog::OnLbnSelchangeWordList()
{
        // TODO: Add your control notification handler code here
        CString Line;
        pE = reinterpret_cast<CEdit
*>(GetDlgItem(IDC_SELECTED_WORD));
        pLB = reinterpret_cast<CListBox
*>(GetDlgItem(IDC_WORD_LIST));
        int i = pLB->GetCurSel(); int n = pLB->GetTextLen(i);
        pLB->GetText(i, Line.GetBuffer(n));
        Line.ReleaseBuffer(); pE->SetWindowText(Line.GetBuffer(0));
        global_StrSelectedWord = Line;

}

CString CInputWordDialog::GetSelectedWord()
{
        return global_StrSelectedWord;

}


void CInputWordDialog::OnBnClickedAddWord()
{
        // TODO: Add your control notification handler code here
            int n; CString Data, Data2, FileName;
              pE = reinterpret_cast<CEdit
*>(GetDlgItem(IDC_SELECTED_WORD));
              pLB = reinterpret_cast<CListBox
*>(GetDlgItem(IDC_WORD_LIST));
              for(int i=0; i<pLB->GetCount(); i++)
              {
                    n = pLB->GetTextLen(i); pLB-
>GetText(i,Data2.GetBuffer(n)); pE->GetWindowTextA(Data);
```

```
            if(Data==Data2)
            {
                pLB->SelectString(i, Data);
                AfxMessageBox("Word already exists in
List");
                pE->SetWindowTextA(_T(""));
                return;
            }
        }

        FileName = "WordList.dat";
        if(!ObjF.Open(FileName, CStdioFile:: modeCreate |
CStdioFile::modeNoTruncate | CStdioFile::modeReadWrite))    ///to
create file or check if already exists
        {}
        pE->GetWindowTextA(Data); Data+="\n";
        ObjF.SeekToEnd(); ObjF.WriteString(Data);
        ObjF.Close();
        pE->SetWindowTextA(_T(""));

        pLB->ResetContent();
        ObjF.Open("WordList.dat", CStdioFile::modeRead);
        ObjF.SeekToBegin();
        while(ObjF.ReadString(Data)!=NULL)    pLB-
>AddString(Data);
        ObjF.Close();
}
```

CHAPTER 6

HEADER FILES

```cpp
// ChildFrm.h : interface of the CChildFrame class

#if !defined(AFX_CHILDFRM_H__7DCF8BCA_A1D5_11D9_8412_0050BFE4C25D__INCLUDED_)
#define AFX_CHILDFRM_H__7DCF8BCA_A1D5_11D9_8412_0050BFE4C25D__INCLUDED_

#if _MSC_VER > 1000
#pragma once
#endif // _MSC_VER > 1000


class CChildFrame : public CMDIChildWnd
{
	DECLARE_DYNCREATE(CChildFrame)
public:
	CChildFrame();

// Attributes
public:
	CStatusBar m_StatusBar;
	CWnd* m_pWnd;
// Operations
protected:
public:
	virtual BOOL PreCreateWindow(CREATESTRUCT& cs);
public:
	virtual ~CChildFrame();
#ifdef _DEBUG
	virtual void AssertValid() const;
	virtual void Dump(CDumpContext& dc) const;
#endif

// Generated message map functions
protected:
	//{{AFX_MSG(CChildFrame)
	afx_msg int OnCreate(LPCREATESTRUCT lpCreateStruct);
	//}}AFX_MSG
	DECLARE_MESSAGE_MAP()
};


#endif // !defined(AFX_CHILDFRM_H__7DCF8BCA_A1D5_11D9_8412_0050BFE4C25D__INCLUDED_)
```

```cpp
// DataFile.h: interface for the CDataFile class.

#if !defined(AFX_DATAFILE_H__D140F9C0_9BC4_11D6_ABE1_0011D87A3DF6__INCLUDED_)
#define AFX_DATAFILE_H__D140F9C0_9BC4_11D6_ABE1_0011D87A3DF6__INCLUDED_

#if _MSC_VER > 1000
#pragma once
#endif // _MSC_VER > 1000

class CDataFile : public CObject
{
protected:

public:
      CDataFile();
      virtual ~CDataFile();

//    CList<CPoint, const CPoint&> m_PointList2;
      CStdioFile tryTextFile;
      char *xstr, *ystr;


};

#endif // !defined(AFX_DATAFILE_H__D140F9C0_9BC4_11D6_ABE1_0011D87A3DF6__INCLUDED_)
```

```cpp
#if !defined(Elements_h)
#define Elements_h

class CElement : public CObject
{

DECLARE_SERIAL(CElement)
protected:
      COLORREF m_Color;
      CRect m_EnclosingRect;
      int m_Pen;
      int m_PenStyle;


public:
      virtual ~CElement(){}
      virtual void Draw(CDC* pDC, const CElement* pElement = 0) const{}
      virtual void Move(const CSize& Size){}

      CRect GetBoundRect() const;

      virtual void Serialize(CArchive& ar);

protected:
      CElement(){}

};


class CLine : public CElement
{
DECLARE_SERIAL(CLine)
public:
      virtual void Draw(CDC* pDC, const CElement* pElement = 0) const;
      virtual void Move(const CSize& Size);

      CLine(const CPoint& Start, const CPoint& End,
            const COLORREF& Color, int PenStyle, const int& PenWidth);
      virtual void Serialize(CArchive& ar);
protected:
      CPoint m_StartPoint;
      CPoint m_EndPoint;

      CLine(){}

};

class CRectangle : public CElement
{
DECLARE_SERIAL(CRectangle)
public:
      virtual void Draw(CDC* pDC, const CElement* pElement = 0) const;
```

```cpp
        virtual void Move(const CSize& Size);

        CRectangle(const CPoint& Start, const CPoint& End,
              const COLORREF& Color, int PenStyle, const int&
PenWidth);
        virtual void Serialize(CArchive& ar);
protected:

        CRectangle(){}

};

class CCircle : public CElement
{
DECLARE_SERIAL(CCircle)
public:
        virtual void Draw(CDC* pDC, const CElement* pElement = 0)
const;
        virtual void Move(const CSize& Size);

        CCircle(const CPoint& Start, const CPoint& End,
              const COLORREF& Color, int PenStyle, const int&
PenWidth);
        virtual void Serialize(CArchive& ar);
protected:

        CCircle(){}

};

class CCurve : public CElement
{
DECLARE_SERIAL(CCurve)
public:
        CCurve();
        ~CCurve();
        virtual void Draw(CDC* pDC, const CElement* pElement = 0)
const;
        virtual void Move(const CSize& Size);

        CCurve(const CPoint& m_FirstPoint, const CPoint&
m_SecondPoint,
              const COLORREF& Color, int PenStyle, const int&
PenWidth);

        void AddSegment(const CPoint& Point);
        virtual void Serialize(CArchive& ar);

        void temp();

protected:

        CList<CPoint, const CPoint&> m_PointList;


        //CCurve();
        //~CCurve();
```

```
};

class CEllipse : public CElement
{
DECLARE_SERIAL(CEllipse)
public:
      virtual void Draw(CDC* pDC, const CElement* pElement = 0) const;
      virtual void Move(const CSize& Size);

      CEllipse(const CPoint& Start, const CPoint& End,
            const COLORREF& Color, int PenStyle, const int& PenWidth);
      virtual void Serialize(CArchive& ar);
protected:

      CEllipse(){}

};

class CText : public CElement
{
DECLARE_SERIAL(CText)
public:
      virtual void Draw(CDC* pDC, const CElement* pElement = 0) const;

      virtual void Move(const CSize& Size);
      CText(const CPoint& Start, const CPoint& End,
            const CString& String, const COLORREF& Color,
            int PenStyle, const int& PenWidth);
      virtual void Serialize(CArchive& ar);
protected:

      CPoint m_StartPoint;
      CString m_String;
      CText(){}

};

#endif
```

```c
// Graph.h: interface for the CGraph class.

#if !defined(AFX_GRAPH_H__609A0660_9D5B_11D6_ABE1_0011D87A3DF6__INCLUDED_)
#define AFX_GRAPH_H__609A0660_9D5B_11D6_ABE1_0011D87A3DF6__INCLUDED_

#if _MSC_VER > 1000
#pragma once
#endif // _MSC_VER > 1000

// Some  defines

//colorschemes
#define G_DEFAULTSCHEME 0
#define G_WHITESCHEME 1
#define G_REDSCHEME 2
#define G_BLUESCHEME 3
#define G_GREENSCHEME 4
#define G_MAGENTASCHEME 5
#define G_YELLOWSCHEME 6
#define G_CYANSCHEME 7

//default graphsize
#define G_MINGRAPHWIDTH 750//500   //350
#define G_MINGRAPHHEIGHT 400//300   //200

//default axies scaling
#define G_DEFAULTXMIN 0    //-100
#define G_DEFAULTXMAX 500  //100
#define G_DEFAULTYMIN -300  //100
#define G_DEFAULTYMAX 0    //100

//miscellaneous
#define G_NUMTICKSANDGRID 10 //how may parts the dataarea is divided
#define G_TICKLENGTH 10 //size of those little ticks on the axes

/*
Function related  defines and stuff
*/
//for the builtin functions
#define NUMFUNCTIONS 12
#define G_XSQUARED    0
#define G_XCUBED 1
#define G_MXPLUSC     2
#define G_SINX       3
#define G_COSX       4
#define G_LOGEX      5
//Plot function
#define G_PLOTXY 6
#define G_PLOTDEV_PERCENT      7
#define G_PLOTDEV_ABS 8
#define G_MULTIPLOTXY 9
#define G_HISTOGRAM_PERCENT 10
#define G_HISTOGRAM_ABS 11
```

```c
#define G_GRAPH 12

//plot type bar,line, etc...
#define NUMCHARTTYPES 3
#define G_BARCHART 0 //a rect (may be one pixel thick)
#define G_LINECHART 1 // each point is a line drawn from each x-y point to the next
#define G_DOTCHART 2 //a dot is placed at X-Y

#define G_BARCHARTWIDTH 5 //default width of a bar chart

//the colors for multiplot graphs
#define G_NUM_MULTIPLOT_COLORS 8
#define G_MULTIPLOT_COLOR_ONE (RGB(192,255,255))
#define G_MULTIPLOT_COLOR_TWO (RGB(0,0,255))
#define G_MULTIPLOT_COLOR_THREE (RGB(255,0,0))
#define G_MULTIPLOT_COLOR_FOUR (RGB(255,255,0))
#define G_MULTIPLOT_COLOR_FIVE (RGB(255,192,192))
#define G_MULTIPLOT_COLOR_SIX (RGB(0,255,0))
#define G_MULTIPLOT_COLOR_SEVEN (RGB(0,255,255))
#define G_MULTIPLOT_COLOR_EIGHT (RGB(255,0,255))


//some structures for passing data
typedef struct
{
    UINT FuncType;//e.g G_SINX
    UINT ChartType;//bar,line, dot etc..
    double xMin;
    double xMax;
    double yMin;
    double yMax;
    char   *szGraphTitle;
    char   *szYLegend;
    char *szXLegend;
    double *pPlotXYItems;
    UINT    num_PlotXYItems;
    double  Const_1;
    double Const_2;
}G_FUNCTIONSTRUCT, *LPG_FUNCTIONSTRUCT;

typedef struct
{
    double xFloat;
    double yFloat;
}CFloatPoint;

static int m_FileLine;
class CGraph
{
public:
    void AddToFloatList(double,double);

    CString LoopText(CString);
    void ShowTicks(BOOL bShow);
    void ClearFunction(void);
```

```cpp
    BOOL DoFunction(G_FUNCTIONSTRUCT *pFunctionParams);
    void SetFunctionName(CString FunctionName);
    void ShowGrid(BOOL bShow);
    void SetYLineAtLeft(BOOL AtLeft);
    void GraphSetAllDefaults();
    void SetYLegendText(CString YText);
    void SetXLegendText(CString XText);
    void SetGraphTitle(CString GraphTitle);
    void PaintGraph(void);
    CGraph(CWnd *pParentWnd,int xPos=0, int yPos=0, int Width
=0, int Height=0, UINT colorscheme=G_BLUESCHEME);
    void SetYAxisScale(double min, double max);
    void SetXAxisScale(double min,double max);
    void SetGraphSizePos(int xPos, int yPos, int Width, int
Height);
    void SetColorScheme(int Scheme, BOOL bRedraw=FALSE);
    void CreateGraphFont(CString FaceName,UINT size);
    CGraph();
    virtual ~CGraph();

    ///for UNIPEN Files
    int GetUnipenData(CString);
    void AdjustUnipenDataList(CList<CFloatPoint, const
CFloatPoint&>*);

public:
    UINT m_GraphType;
    CList<CFloatPoint, const CFloatPoint&> m_graphPointList;
    void DoCurve();
    CStdioFile m_GraphTextFile;
private:

    char *xstr, *ystr;
    CList<CPoint, const CPoint&> m_GraphList;
    //   void DoHistogram();
    LONG ConvertToGraphCoords(double x, double y);
    COLORREF GetMultiPlotPenColor(UINT PenNumber);
    void CGraph::DoDeviationPercentAbs(void);
    double ConstrainY (double y);
    void DrawConnectLine(UINT FromX, UINT FromY, UINT ToX, UINT
ToY);
    void PlotPoints(UINT x, UINT y, UINT prevx, UINT prevy);
    void DrawDot (UINT X, UINT Y);
    void DrawFunction();
    void SetDefaultColorScheme(void);
    void DrawFunctionName(void);
    void SetDefaultFunctionName(void);
    CString m_szFunctionNameText;
    COLORREF m_crFunctionNameColor;
    void DrawYAxisNumbers();
    void DrawXAxisNumbers(void);
    void DrawTicks(void);
    double CalcYAxisGridAndTicks(void);
    CRect CalcDataArea(void);
    double CalcXAxisGridAndTicks(void);
    void DrawGrid(void);
    void DrawYLegend();
```

```cpp
        void DrawXLegend();
        void SetDefaultYLegend(void);
        void SetDefaultXLegend(void);
        void SetDefaultGraphTitle(void);
        void DrawGraphTitle();
        UINT CalcRightMargin();
        UINT CalcLeftMargin();
        UINT CalcBottomMargin();
        UINT CalcTopMargin();
        BOOL m_bShowTicks;//Ticks are the little things on the x & y axis
        BOOL m_bShowGrid;
        BOOL m_bAutofit;
        BOOL m_bYLineAtLeft;
        CString m_szFontFace;
        CString m_szYLegendText;
        CString m_szXLegendText;
        CString m_szGraphTitle;
        COLORREF m_crYTickColor;
        COLORREF m_crXTickColor;
        COLORREF m_crYLegendTextColor;
        COLORREF m_crXLegendTextColor;
        COLORREF m_crGraphTitleColor;
        COLORREF m_crGraphPenColor;
        COLORREF m_crGraphBkColor;
        COLORREF m_crGridColor;
        int m_iFontSize;//
        int m_iGraphWidth;//
        int m_iGraphHeight;//
        int m_iGraphX;//location of the graph within the window
        int m_iGraphY;//location of the graph within the window
        double m_dXAxisMin;// the start value of X
        double m_dYAxisMin;//start value of Y
        double m_dXAxisMax;
        double m_dYAxisMax;
        CWnd *m_pWnd;//parent/owner
        CFont m_GraphFont;//default font font created from default fontface, & point size
        int m_iCharHeight;//calculated from the font
        int m_iCharWidth;//calculated from the font
        int m_iOriginX;//location of the origin within the graph
        int m_iOriginY;//location of the origin within the graph
        double m_dPixelsPerY;//scaling
        double m_dPixelsPerX;//scaling
        int m_iScrollPosX;//
        int m_iScrollPosY;//
        //Data related variables
        G_FUNCTIONSTRUCT *m_pFunctionParams;

};

#endif //
!defined(AFX_GRAPH_H__609A0660_9D5B_11D6_ABE1_0011D87A3DF6__INCLUDED_)
```

```cpp
#if !defined(AFX_GRAPHDIALOG_H__87E2EF80_9FB2_11D6_ABE1_0011D87A3DF6__INCLUDED_)
#define AFX_GRAPHDIALOG_H__87E2EF80_9FB2_11D6_ABE1_0011D87A3DF6__INCLUDED_

#include "Graph.h"
#if _MSC_VER > 1000
#pragma once
#endif // _MSC_VER > 1000
// GraphDialog.h : header file

class CGraphDialog : public CDialog
{
// Construction
public:
    double *m_pPlotItems;
    LPG_FUNCTIONSTRUCT m_lpfs;
    CGraph *m_pGraph;

    CGraphDialog(CWnd* pParent = NULL);   // standard constructor
    void ToCallOnGraph();
// Dialog Data
    //{{AFX_DATA(CGraphDialog)
    enum { IDD = 144 };
    int m_Scale;
    protected:
    virtual void DoDataExchange(CDataExchange* pDX);    // DDX/DDV support
protected:
    HICON m_hIcon;
    CListBox* pListBox;
    CString m_ListDataStr;
    CStdioFile m_PointRecordFileXls;
    void AddToListBox();
    virtual BOOL OnInitDialog();
    afx_msg void OnSysCommand(UINT nID, LPARAM lParam);
    afx_msg void OnPaint();
    afx_msg void OnDestroy();
    afx_msg void OnGraph();
    afx_msg void OnOriginal();
    afx_msg void OnSizeCenter();
    afx_msg void OnInterpolation();
    afx_msg void OnSlantCorrection();
    afx_msg void OnSmooth();
    afx_msg void OnResampling();
    afx_msg void OnClearGraph();
    afx_msg void OnFEResults();
    afx_msg void OnNextCharacter();
    afx_msg void OnCloseExit();
    //}}AFX_MSG
    DECLARE_MESSAGE_MAP()
};
```

```
#endif //
!defined(AFX_GRAPHDIALOG_H__87E2EF80_9FB2_11D6_ABE1_0011D87A3DF6_
_INCLUDED_)
```

```cpp
// HWRAnuj.h : main header file for the HWRAnuj application
//

#if !defined(AFX_HWRAnuj_H__7DCF8BC4_A1D5_11D9_8412_0050BFE4C25D__INCLUDED_)
#define AFX_HWRAnuj_H__7DCF8BC4_A1D5_11D9_8412_0050BFE4C25D__INCLUDED_

#if _MSC_VER > 1000
#pragma once
#endif // _MSC_VER > 1000

#ifndef __AFXWIN_H__
    #error include 'stdafx.h' before including this file for PCH
#endif

#include "resource.h"       // main symbols

// CHWRAnujApp:
// See HWRAnuj.cpp for the implementation of this class
//
#include "OurConstants.h"
class CHWRAnujApp : public CWinApp
{
public:
    CHWRAnujApp();

// Overrides
    // ClassWizard generated virtual function overrides
    //{{AFX_VIRTUAL(CHWRAnujApp)
    public:
    virtual BOOL InitInstance();
    //}}AFX_VIRTUAL

// Implementation
    //{{AFX_MSG(CHWRAnujApp)
    afx_msg void OnAppAbout();
    // NOTE - the ClassWizard will add and remove member functions here.
        //    DO NOT EDIT what you see in these blocks of generated code !
    //}}AFX_MSG
    DECLARE_MESSAGE_MAP()
};


#endif // !defined(AFX_HWRAnuj_H__7DCF8BC4_A1D5_11D9_8412_0050BFE4C25D__INCLUDED_)
```

```cpp
// HWRAnujDoc.h : interface of the CHWRAnujDoc class
#if !defined(AFX_HWRAnujDOC_H__7DCF8BCC_A1D5_11D9_8412_0050BFE4C25D__INCLUDED_)
#define AFX_HWRAnujDOC_H__7DCF8BCC_A1D5_11D9_8412_0050BFE4C25D__INCLUDED_

#if _MSC_VER > 1000
#pragma once
#endif // _MSC_VER > 1000


class CHWRAnujDoc : public CDocument
{
protected: // create from serialization only
    CHWRAnujDoc();
    DECLARE_DYNCREATE(CHWRAnujDoc)


// Attributes
public:

    WORD GetElementType() const
    {return m_Element;}

    COLORREF GetElementColor() const
    {return m_Color;}

    int GetPenStyle() const
    {return m_PenStyle;}

    void AddElement(CElement* pElement)
    {m_ElementList.AddTail(pElement);SetModifiedFlag();}

    int GetPenWidth() const
    {return m_PenWidth;}

    POSITION GetListHeadPosition() const
    {return m_ElementList.GetHeadPosition();}

    CElement* GetNext(POSITION& aPos) const
    {return m_ElementList.GetNext(aPos);}

    POSITION GetListTailPosition() const
    {return m_ElementList.GetTailPosition();}

    CElement* GetPrev(POSITION& aPos) const
    {return m_ElementList.GetPrev(aPos);}

    void DeleteElement(CElement* pElement);
    void DeleteAllElements();
    void SendToBack(CElement* pElement);

    CSize GetDocSize() const
    {return m_DocSize;}

// Operations
```

```cpp
public:

// Overrides
    // ClassWizard generated virtual function overrides
    //{{AFX_VIRTUAL(CHWRAnujDoc)
    public:
    virtual BOOL OnNewDocument();
    virtual void Serialize(CArchive& ar);
    //}}AFX_VIRTUAL

// Implementation
public:
    virtual ~CHWRAnujDoc();
#ifdef _DEBUG
    virtual void AssertValid() const;
    virtual void Dump(CDumpContext& dc) const;
#endif

protected:

// Generated message map functions
    COLORREF m_Color;
    WORD m_Element;
    int m_PenStyle;
    int m_PenWidth;

    CSize m_DocSize;
    CTypedPtrList<CObList, CElement*> m_ElementList;

protected:
    //{{AFX_MSG(CHWRAnujDoc)
    afx_msg void OnColorBlack();
    afx_msg void OnColorBlue();
    afx_msg void OnColorGreen();
    afx_msg void OnColorRed();
    afx_msg void OnElementCircle();
    afx_msg void OnElementCurve();
    afx_msg void OnElementLine();
    afx_msg void OnElementRectangle();
    afx_msg void OnUpdateColorBlack(CCmdUI* pCmdUI);
    afx_msg void OnUpdateColorBlue(CCmdUI* pCmdUI);
    afx_msg void OnUpdateColorGreen(CCmdUI* pCmdUI);
    afx_msg void OnUpdateColorRed(CCmdUI* pCmdUI);
    afx_msg void OnUpdateElementCircle(CCmdUI* pCmdUI);
    afx_msg void OnUpdateElementCurve(CCmdUI* pCmdUI);
    afx_msg void OnUpdateElementLine(CCmdUI* pCmdUI);
    afx_msg void OnUpdateElementRectangle(CCmdUI* pCmdUI);
    afx_msg void OnElementEllipse();
    afx_msg void OnUpdateElementEllipse(CCmdUI* pCmdUI);
    afx_msg void OnPenSolid();
    afx_msg void OnUpdatePenSolid(CCmdUI* pCmdUI);
    afx_msg void OnPenDot();
    afx_msg void OnUpdatePenDot(CCmdUI* pCmdUI);
    afx_msg void OnPenDashed();
    afx_msg void OnUpdatePenDashed(CCmdUI* pCmdUI);
    afx_msg void OnPenDashdotdot();
    afx_msg void OnUpdatePenDashdotdot(CCmdUI* pCmdUI);
```

```
        afx_msg void OnPenDashdot();
        afx_msg void OnUpdatePenDashdot(CCmdUI* pCmdUI);
        afx_msg void OnPenwidth();
        afx_msg void OnElementText();
        afx_msg void OnUpdateElementText(CCmdUI* pCmdUI);
        //}}AFX_MSG
        DECLARE_MESSAGE_MAP()
};

//{{AFX_INSERT_LOCATION}}

#endif //
!defined(AFX_HWRAnujDOC_H__7DCF8BCC_A1D5_11D9_8412_0050BFE4C25D__INCLUDED_)
```

```cpp
// HWRAnujView.h : interface of the CHWRAnujView class

#if !defined(AFX_HWRAnujVIEW_H__7DCF8BCE_A1D5_11D9_8412_0050BFE4C25D__INCLUDED_)
#define AFX_HWRAnujVIEW_H__7DCF8BCE_A1D5_11D9_8412_0050BFE4C25D__INCLUDED_

#if _MSC_VER > 1000
#pragma once
#endif // _MSC_VER > 1000
#include "Preprocessing.h"

typedef struct{
    double xMin, xMax, yMin, yMax;
    int SR;   ///Stroke Result
}CWordR;

class CHWRAnujView : public CScrollView
{
protected: // create from serialization only
//    CHWRAnujView();
    DECLARE_DYNCREATE(CHWRAnujView)

// Attributes
public:
    CHWRAnujDoc* GetDocument();
    CHWRAnujView();

    CArray<CPointNormalized, const CPointNormalized&> m_Array;
    CStdioFile m_RRLog;

    void GetImageRect(CRect);
// Operations
public:

// Overrides
    // ClassWizard generated virtual function overrides
    //{{AFX_VIRTUAL(CHWRAnujView)
    public:
    virtual void OnDraw(CDC* pDC);  // overridden to draw this view
    virtual BOOL PreCreateWindow(CREATESTRUCT& cs);
    virtual void OnInitialUpdate();
    virtual void OnPrepareDC(CDC* pDC, CPrintInfo* pInfo = NULL);
    protected:
    virtual BOOL OnPreparePrinting(CPrintInfo* pInfo);
    virtual void OnBeginPrinting(CDC* pDC, CPrintInfo* pInfo);
    virtual void OnEndPrinting(CDC* pDC, CPrintInfo* pInfo);
    virtual void OnUpdate(CView* pSender, LPARAM lHint, CObject* pHint);
    //}}AFX_VIRTUAL

// Implementation
public:
```

```cpp
        void ResetScrollSizes();
        virtual ~CHWRAnujView();
#ifdef _DEBUG
        virtual void AssertValid() const;
        virtual void Dump(CDumpContext& dc) const;
#endif

protected:

        CElement* CreateElement();
        CElement* SelectElement(CPoint apoint);
        void MoveElement(CClientDC& aDC, const CPoint& point);

        CPoint m_FirstPoint;
        CPoint m_SecondPoint;
        CElement* m_pTempElement;
        CElement* m_pSelected;

        BOOL m_MoveMode;
        CPoint m_CursorPos;
        CPoint m_FirstPos;

        int m_Scale, m_Result, m_I, m_CEdit_Line, m_Method, m_WordR, m_S12;
        long int m_files, m_segments, m_chars, m_chars4;
        unsigned long int m_CharID;
        char m_CharIDStr[20]; CString m_Character, m_CharStr;
        double m_HLMinX, m_HLMaxX, m_HLMinY, m_HLMaxY;

        CList<CPoint, const CPoint&> m_PointListXY;
        CArray<CPoint, const CPoint&> m_PointArray;
        CString FileName, OFileName, FilePath, Data;
        CStdioFile ObjF, ObjOF;
        CPreprocessing ObjPP;

protected:
        void ListToArray();
        CString GetHandwrittenPoints();
        // Generated message map functions
protected:
        //{{AFX_MSG(CHWRAnujView)
        afx_msg void OnLButtonDown(UINT nFlags, CPoint point);
        afx_msg void OnLButtonUp(UINT nFlags, CPoint point);
        afx_msg void OnMouseMove(UINT nFlags, CPoint point);
        afx_msg void OnCancelMode();
        afx_msg void OnMove();
        afx_msg void OnDelete();
        afx_msg void OnRButtonUp(UINT nFlags, CPoint point);
        afx_msg void OnRButtonDown(UINT nFlags, CPoint point);
        afx_msg void OnSendtoback();
        afx_msg void OnViewScale();
        afx_msg void OnAddFile();
        afx_msg void OnFileNew();
        afx_msg void OnAddFileConfirm();
        afx_msg void OnCollectCancel();
        afx_msg void OnInputWord();
```

```
        afx_msg void OnPreprocessing();
        //}}AFX_MSG
        DECLARE_MESSAGE_MAP()

public:
        //afx_msg void OnAddFile();

};

#ifndef _DEBUG  // debug version in HWRAnujView.cpp
inline CHWRAnujDoc* CHWRAnujView::GetDocument()
   { return (CHWRAnujDoc*)m_pDocument; }
#endif

#endif //
!defined(AFX_HWRAnujVIEW_H__7DCF8BCE_A1D5_11D9_8412_0050BFE4C25D_
_INCLUDED_)
```

```cpp
#pragma once


// CInputWordDialog dialog

class CInputWordDialog : public CDialog
{
    DECLARE_DYNAMIC(CInputWordDialog)

public:
    CInputWordDialog(CWnd* pParent = NULL);   // standard constructor
    virtual ~CInputWordDialog();

// Dialog Data
    //enum { IDD = IDD_INPUT_WORD };
    enum { IDD = 139 };
    CString m_Word, m_SelectedWord;

protected:
    virtual void DoDataExchange(CDataExchange* pDX);    // DDX/DDV support
    virtual BOOL OnInitDialog();
    CStdioFile ObjF;
    CListBox *pLB; CFont *pFont, *pFont2; CEdit *pE;

    DECLARE_MESSAGE_MAP()
public:
    CString GetSelectedWord();

public:
    afx_msg void OnLbnSelchangeWordList();
public:
    afx_msg void OnBnClickedAddWord();
};
```

```cpp
// MainFrm.h : interface of the CMainFrame class

#if !defined(AFX_MAINFRM_H__7DCF8BC8_A1D5_11D9_8412_0050BFE4C25D__INCLUDED_)
#define AFX_MAINFRM_H__7DCF8BC8_A1D5_11D9_8412_0050BFE4C25D__INCLUDED_

#if _MSC_VER > 1000
#pragma once
#endif // _MSC_VER > 1000

class CMainFrame : public CMDIFrameWnd
{
    DECLARE_DYNAMIC(CMainFrame)
public:
    CMainFrame();

// Attributes
public:

// Operations
public:

// Overrides
    // ClassWizard generated virtual function overrides
    //{{AFX_VIRTUAL(CMainFrame)
    virtual BOOL PreCreateWindow(CREATESTRUCT& cs);
    //}}AFX_VIRTUAL

// Implementation
public:
    void SetPaneText(int Pane, LPCTSTR Text);
    virtual ~CMainFrame();
#ifdef _DEBUG
    virtual void AssertValid() const;
    virtual void Dump(CDumpContext& dc) const;
#endif

protected:  // control bar embedded members
    CStatusBar  m_wndStatusBar;
    CToolBar    m_wndToolBar;

// Generated message map functions
protected:
    //{{AFX_MSG(CMainFrame)
    afx_msg int OnCreate(LPCREATESTRUCT lpCreateStruct);
    //}}AFX_MSG
    DECLARE_MESSAGE_MAP()
};


#endif // !defined(AFX_MAINFRM_H__7DCF8BC8_A1D5_11D9_8412_0050BFE4C25D__INCLUDED_)
```

```cpp
#ifndef OurConstants_h
#define OurConstants_h

const WORD LINE = 101U;
const WORD RECTANGLE = 102U;
const WORD CIRCLE = 103U;
const WORD CURVE = 104U;
const WORD ELLIPSE = 105U;
const WORD TEXT = 106U;

const COLORREF BLACK = RGB(0,0,0);
const COLORREF RED = RGB(255,0,0);
const COLORREF GREEN = RGB(0,255,0);
const COLORREF BLUE = RGB(0,0,255);
const COLORREF SELECT_COLOR = RGB(255,0,180);

const int SOLID = PS_SOLID;
const int DASH = PS_DASH;
const int DOT = PS_DOT;
const int DASHDOT = PS_DASHDOT;
const int DASHDOTDOT = PS_DASHDOTDOT;

const UINT VERSION_NUMBER=1;

const int ARR_SIZE=40;
const int ENGLISH=0; //0 for Gurmukhi, 1 for English

#endif
```

```cpp
#if !defined(AFX_PENDIALOG_H__2F19A1E0_B4F0_11D9_8412_0050BFE4C25D__INCLUDED_)
#define AFX_PENDIALOG_H__2F19A1E0_B4F0_11D9_8412_0050BFE4C25D__INCLUDED_

#if _MSC_VER > 1000
#pragma once
#endif // _MSC_VER > 1000
// PenDialog.h : header file
//

// CPenDialog dialog

class CPenDialog : public CDialog
{
// Construction
public:
	CPenDialog(CWnd* pParent = NULL);   // standard constructor

// Dialog Data
	//{{AFX_DATA(CPenDialog)
	enum { IDD = IDD_PENWIDTH_DLG };
		// NOTE: the ClassWizard will add data members here
	//}}AFX_DATA


// Overrides
	// ClassWizard generated virtual function overrides
	//{{AFX_VIRTUAL(CPenDialog)
	protected:
	virtual void DoDataExchange(CDataExchange* pDX);    // DDX/DDV support
	//}}AFX_VIRTUAL

// Implementation
public:
	int m_PenWidth;         //Record the Pen Width

protected:

	// Generated message map functions
	//{{AFX_MSG(CPenDialog)
	virtual BOOL OnInitDialog();
	afx_msg void OnCancelMode();
	afx_msg void OnPenwidth0();
	afx_msg void OnPenwidth1();
	afx_msg void OnPenwidth2();
	afx_msg void OnPenwidth3();
	afx_msg void OnPenwidth4();
	afx_msg void OnPenwidth5();
	//}}AFX_MSG
	DECLARE_MESSAGE_MAP()
};

//{{AFX_INSERT_LOCATION}}
```

```
// Microsoft Visual C++ will insert additional declarations
immediately before the previous line.

#endif //
!defined(AFX_PENDIALOG_H__2F19A1E0_B4F0_11D9_8412_0050BFE4C25D__I
NCLUDED_)
```

```cpp
// Preprocessing.h: interface for the CPreprocessing class.

#if !defined(AFX_PREPROCESSING_H__DBF40122_C229_11DA_ABB2_0011D87A3DF6__INCLUDED_)
#define AFX_PREPROCESSING_H__DBF40122_C229_11DA_ABB2_0011D87A3DF6__INCLUDED_

#if _MSC_VER > 1000
#pragma once
#endif // _MSC_VER > 1000
//#include "Feature.h"

class CPreprocessing : public CObject
{
public:
    CPreprocessing();
    virtual ~CPreprocessing();

    int AddToPPList(CList<CPoint, const CPoint&>*);
    double CalculateSlope(CPointNormalized&, CPointNormalized&);
    double Distance(CPointNormalized&, CPointNormalized&);
    double Round(double Value, int Precision);
    void SizeCentering2();
    CArray<CPointNormalized, const CPointNormalized&> m_PPArray;

public:
    //CFeature ObjFeature;


protected:
    char m_BufferX[20], m_BufferY[20];
    int m_xNor, m_yNor, m_xTextLength, m_yTextLength, m_I, m_pointsBeforePP, m_pointsAfterPP;
    double m_MinX, m_MaxX, m_MinY, m_MaxY, m_Kx, m_Ky, m_DiffX, m_DiffY, m_K, m_FixedY, m_NewXL;
    double m_xFactor, m_yFactor, m_yxRatio;
    double xMax, xMin, yMax, yMin, m_xL, m_yL, m_Factor;
    double xLen, yLen;
    CString m_FileName;
    CArray<CPointNormalized, const CPointNormalized&> m_TempArray2;
    CArray<CPointNormalized, const CPointNormalized&> m_TempArray;

    CStdioFile m_PPTextFile;
protected:
    void BSpline();
    void BSplineFormula(CPointNormalized&, CPointNormalized&, CPointNormalized&, CPointNormalized&);
    void CalculateMaxMinText();
    void Centering();
    double ChainCodeMethod(int, int);
    void CreateTextFile(CString);
    void EquiStraightLines();
    void EqualDistance(int, int);
```

```
        void Equidistancing();
        void EquiDistantPoints();
        void EquiDistantPointsNotFixed();
        void FilterClosePoints();
        void FilterSamePoints();
        double FindStraightLine(int, int, int);
        void GuassianArray(double, double, double, double, double,
int, int);
        double GuassianFormulaX(double, int, int);
        double GuassianFormulaY(double, int, int);
        void GuassianSmoothing();
        void Interpolation();
        void NeighbourMean(int);
        void NeighbouringPoints();
        void NonDecimalPoints();
        void OriginalTextFile();
        void OriginalTextFilePoints();
        void RoundPoints();
        void RoundPointsZero();
        void SizeCentering();
        void SizeNormalization();
        void SlantAdjustment(int, int);
        void SlantCorrectionMethod();
        void SlantCorrection();
        void Smoothing();
        void UpdateArray();
        void UpdateSlant(int, int, double);
};

#endif //
!defined(AFX_PREPROCESSING_H__DBF40122_C229_11DA_ABB2_0011D87A3DF
6__INCLUDED_)
```

```
//{{NO_DEPENDENCIES}}
// Microsoft Visual C++ generated include file.
// Used by HWRAnuj.rc
//
#define IDD_ABOUTBOX                    100
#define IDR_MAINFRAME                   128
#define IDR_SKETCHTYPE                  129
#define IDR_CURSOR_MENU                 130
#define IDD_PENWIDTH_DLG                131
#define IDD_SCALE_DLG                   133
#define IDD_TEXT_DLG                    134
#define IDD_TOOLS_DLG                   135
#define IDB_BITMAP1                     137
#define IDD_INPUT_WORD                  139
#define IDD_GRAPH_DLG                   144
#define IDC_PENWIDTH0                   1000
#define IDC_PENWIDTH1                   1001
#define IDC_PENWIDTH2                   1002
#define IDC_PENWIDTH3                   1003
#define IDC_PENWIDTH4                   1004
#define IDC_PENWIDTH5                   1005
#define IDC_SCALELIST                   1008
#define IDC_EDITTEXT                    1009
#define IDC_DATAFILE                    1010
#define IDC_GRAPHDATALIST               1012
#define IDC_NEXTCHARACTER               1032
#define IDC_WORD_LIST                   1034
#define IDC_SELECTED_WORD               1039
#define IDC_ADD_WORD                    1040
#define IDC_ORIGINAL                    1041
#define IDC_SIZECENTER                  1042
#define IDC_INTERPOLATION               1043
#define IDC_SLANTCORRECTION             1044
#define IDC_SMOOTH                      1045
#define IDC_BUTTON1                     1046
#define IDC_RESAMPLING                  1046
#define ID_ELEMENT_LINE                 32771
#define ID_ELEMENT_RECTANGLE            32772
#define ID_ELEMENT_CIRCLE               32773
#define ID_ELEMENT_CURVE                32774
#define ID_ELEMENT_BLACK                32775
#define ID_ELEMENT_RED                  32776
#define ID_ELEMENT_GREEN                32777
#define ID_ELEMENT_BLUE                 32778
#define ID_COLOR_BLACK                  32779
#define ID_COLOR_RED                    32780
#define ID_COLOR_GREEN                  32781
#define ID_COLOR_BLUE                   32782
#define ID_ELEMENT_ELLIPSE              32787
#define ID_PEN_SOLID                    32790
#define ID_PEN_DASHED                   32791
#define ID_PEN_DOT                      32792
#define ID_PEN_DASHDOT                  32793
#define ID_PEN_DASHDOTDOT               32794
#define ID_MOVE                         32795
#define ID_DELETE                       32796
#define ID_SENDTOBACK                   32797
```

```
#define ID_PENWIDTH                     32798
#define ID_VIEW_SCALE                   32801
#define ID_ELEMENT_TEXT                 32802
#define ID_RECOGNIZE_DATAPP             32803
#define ID_RECOGNIZE_TRY                32804
#define ID_ADD_FILE                     32805
#define ID_BUILD_NORMALIZE              32806
#define ID_BUILD_DATACOLLECTION         32807
#define ID_RECOGNITION                  32808
#define ID_DOT                          32813
#define ID_HMMStart                     32815
#define ID_ElasticMatching              32816
#define ID_SLS                          32817
#define ID_HMM                          32818
#define ID_RRLog                        32819
#define ID_WORDR                        32820
#define ID_WordRecognition              32821
#define ID_BUTTON32822                  32822
#define ID_AboveHLBindi                 32823
#define ID_ADD_FILE_CONFIRM             32824
#define ID_FORM_SLS                     32825
#define ID_COLLECT_CANCEL               32827
#define ID_INPUT_WORD                   32828
#define ID_Preprocessing                32829

// Next default values for new objects
//
#ifdef APSTUDIO_INVOKED
#ifndef APSTUDIO_READONLY_SYMBOLS
#define _APS_3D_CONTROLS                       1
#define _APS_NEXT_RESOURCE_VALUE        145
#define _APS_NEXT_COMMAND_VALUE         32830
#define _APS_NEXT_CONTROL_VALUE         1047
#define _APS_NEXT_SYMED_VALUE           101
#endif
#endif
```

```cpp
#if !defined(AFX_SCALEDIALOG_H__83F08F00_B65B_11D9_8412_0050BFE4C25D__INCLUDED_)
#define AFX_SCALEDIALOG_H__83F08F00_B65B_11D9_8412_0050BFE4C25D__INCLUDED_

#if _MSC_VER > 1000
#pragma once
#endif // _MSC_VER > 1000
// ScaleDialog.h : header file
// CScaleDialog dialog

class CScaleDialog : public CDialog
{
// Construction
public:
    CScaleDialog(CWnd* pParent = NULL);   // standard constructor

// Dialog Data
    //{{AFX_DATA(CScaleDialog)
    enum { IDD = 133 };
    int     m_Scale;
    //}}AFX_DATA


// Overrides
    // ClassWizard generated virtual function overrides
    //{{AFX_VIRTUAL(CScaleDialog)
    protected:
    virtual void DoDataExchange(CDataExchange* pDX);    // DDX/DDV support
    //}}AFX_VIRTUAL

// Implementation
protected:

    // Generated message map functions
    //{{AFX_MSG(CScaleDialog)
    virtual BOOL OnInitDialog();
    //}}AFX_MSG
    DECLARE_MESSAGE_MAP()
};

//{{AFX_INSERT_LOCATION}}
// Microsoft Visual C++ will insert additional declarations immediately before the previous line.

#endif // !defined(AFX_SCALEDIALOG_H__83F08F00_B65B_11D9_8412_0050BFE4C25D__INCLUDED_)
```

```cpp
// stdafx.h : include file for standard system include files,
#if !defined(AFX_STDAFX_H__7DCF8BC6_A1D5_11D9_8412_0050BFE4C25D__INCLUDED_)
#define AFX_STDAFX_H__7DCF8BC6_A1D5_11D9_8412_0050BFE4C25D__INCLUDED_

#if _MSC_VER > 1000
#pragma once
#endif // _MSC_VER > 1000

#define VC_EXTRALEAN        // Exclude rarely-used stuff from Windows headers

#include <afxwin.h>         // MFC core and standard components
#include <afxext.h>
#include <afxdb.h>
#include<afxtempl.h>        // MFC extensions

typedef struct{
    double x;
    double y;
    int strokeNumber;
}CPointNormalized;
//CPointNormalized is used here provide its access to CNormalize and CFeature classes
#include <afxdisp.h>        // MFC Automation classes
#include <afxdtctl.h>       // MFC support for Internet Explorer 4 Common Controls
#ifndef _AFX_NO_AFXCMN_SUPPORT
#include <afxcmn.h>         // MFC support for Windows Common Controls
#endif // _AFX_NO_AFXCMN_SUPPORT


//{{AFX_INSERT_LOCATION}}
// Microsoft Visual C++ will insert additional declarations immediately before the previous line.

#endif // !defined(AFX_STDAFX_H__7DCF8BC6_A1D5_11D9_8412_0050BFE4C25D__INCLUDED_)
```

```cpp
#if !defined(AFX_TEXTDIALOG_H__83F08F01_B65B_11D9_8412_0050BFE4C25D__INCLUDED_)
#define AFX_TEXTDIALOG_H__83F08F01_B65B_11D9_8412_0050BFE4C25D__INCLUDED_

#if _MSC_VER > 1000
#pragma once
#endif // _MSC_VER > 1000
// TextDialog.h : header file
// CTextDialog dialog

class CTextDialog : public CDialog
{
// Construction
public:
    CTextDialog(CWnd* pParent = NULL);   // standard constructor

// Dialog Data
    //{{AFX_DATA(CTextDialog)
    enum { IDD = 134 };
    CString    m_TextString;
    //}}AFX_DATA


// Overrides
    // ClassWizard generated virtual function overrides
    //{{AFX_VIRTUAL(CTextDialog)
    protected:
    virtual void DoDataExchange(CDataExchange* pDX);    // DDX/DDV support
    //}}AFX_VIRTUAL

// Implementation
protected:

    // Generated message map functions
    //{{AFX_MSG(CTextDialog)
        // NOTE: the ClassWizard will add member functions here
    //}}AFX_MSG
    DECLARE_MESSAGE_MAP()
};

//{{AFX_INSERT_LOCATION}}
// Microsoft Visual C++ will insert additional declarations immediately before the previous line.

#endif // !defined(AFX_TEXTDIALOG_H__83F08F01_B65B_11D9_8412_0050BFE4C25D__INCLUDED_)
```

```cpp
#if !defined(AFX_TOOLSDIALOG_H__77692A00_9B09_11D6_ABE1_0011D87A3DF6__INCLUDED_)
#define AFX_TOOLSDIALOG_H__77692A00_9B09_11D6_ABE1_0011D87A3DF6__INCLUDED_

#if _MSC_VER > 1000
#pragma once
#endif // _MSC_VER > 1000
// ToolsDialog.h : header file

// CToolsDialog dialog

class CToolsDialog : public CDialog
{
// Construction
public:
    CToolsDialog(CWnd* pParent = NULL);   // standard constructor

// Dialog Data
    //{{AFX_DATA(CToolsDialog)
    enum { IDD = 135 };

    // NOTE: the ClassWizard will add data members here
    //}}AFX_DATA


// Overrides
    // ClassWizard generated virtual function overrides
    //{{AFX_VIRTUAL(CToolsDialog)
    protected:
    virtual void DoDataExchange(CDataExchange* pDX);    // DDX/DDV support
    //}}AFX_VIRTUAL

// Implementation
public:

    afx_msg void OnDataFile();
protected:

    // Generated message map functions
    //{{AFX_MSG(CToolsDialog)
    virtual BOOL OnInitDialog();

    //}}AFX_MSG
    DECLARE_MESSAGE_MAP()
};

//{{AFX_INSERT_LOCATION}}
// Microsoft Visual C++ will insert additional declarations immediately before the previous line.
```

```
#endif //
!defined(AFX_TOOLSDIALOG_H__77692A00_9B09_11D6_ABE1_0011D87A3DF6_
_INCLUDED_)
```

Screeshots of Developed DHI

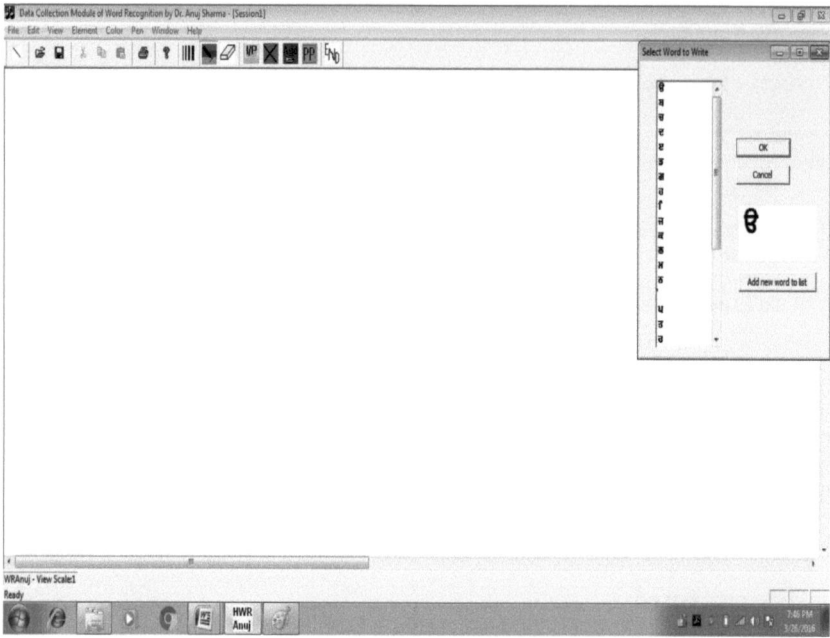

Fig. 6.1 The developed DHI with input dialog where writing word could be selected.

Fig. 6.2 A word written where preprocessing to be done as shown in Fig. 6.3 to 6.5.

Fig. 6.3 A word written where size normalization done in preprocessing for Fig. 6.2.

Fig. 6.4 A word written where text smoothing done in preprocessing for Fig. 6.2.

Fig. 6.5 A word written where resampling of points done in preprocessing for Fig. 6.2.

TABLE OF REFERENCE

1. Anuj Sharma, 2009. Online Handwritten Gurmukhi Character Recognition. PhD Thesis, Thapar University, Patiala, India.
2. Al-Taani, A. T., 2005. An efficient feature extraction algorithm for the recognition of handwritten arabic digits. International Journal of Computational Intelligence, vol. 2, no. 2. pp. 107-111.
3. Artieres, T. and Gallinari, P., 2002. Stroke level HMMs for online handwriting recognition. Proceedings of IWFHR, pp. 227-232.
4. Basu, M., Bunke, H. and Bimbo, A. D., 2005. Guest editors' introduction to the special section on syntactic and structural pattern recognition, IEEE Transactions on Pattern Analysis and Machine Intelligence, vol. 27, no. 7, pp. 1009-1012.
5. Beigi, H., 1996. Pre-processing and dynamics of online handwriting data, feature extraction and recognition. Proceedings of fifth IWFHR, pp. 255-258.
6. Beigi, H., Nathan, K., Clary, G. J., and Subhramonia, J., 1994. Size normalization in unconstrained online handwritng recognition, Proceedings ICIP, pp. 169-173.
7. Bellegarda, E. J., Bellegarda, J. R., Nahamoo, D. and Nathan, K. S., 1994. A fast statistical mixture algorithm for online handwriting recognition. IEEE Transactions on Pattern Analysis and Machine Intelligence, vol. 16, no. 12, pp. 1227-1233.
8. Bellegarda, E. J., Bellegarda, J. R., Namahoo, D. and Nathan K. S., 1993. A probabilistic framework for online handwriting recognition. Proceedings of IWFHR III, pp. 225-234.
9. Bengio, Y., LeCun, Y., Nohl, G. and Burges, C., 1995. LeRec: A NN/HMM hybrid for on-line handwriting recognition. Neural Computation, vol. 7, no. 5, pp. 1289-1303.
10. Biadsy, F., El-Sana, J. and Habash, N., 2006. Online Arabic handwriting recognition using hidden markov models. Proceedings of International Workshop Frontiers of Handwriting Recognition.
11. Blanchard, J., Artieres, T., 2004. Online handwritten documents segmentation. Proceedings of ICFHR. pp. 148-153.

12. Blumenstein, M. and Verma, B., 1999. A new segmentation algorithm for handwritten word recognition. Proceedings of the International Joint Conference on Neural Networks, pp. 878-882.
13. Bontempi, B. and Marcelli, A., 1994. A genetic learning system for on-line character recognition. Proceedings of International Conference on Pattern Recognition, vol. 2, pp. 83-87.
14. Bozinovic, R. M., Srihari, S. N., 1989. Offline cursive script recognition. IEEE Transactions on Pattern Analysis and Machine Intelligence, vol. 2, no. 1, pp. 68-83.
15. Brault, J. J. and Plamondon, R., 1993. Segmenting handwritten signatures at their perceptually important points. IEEE Transactions on Pattern Analysis and Machine Intelligence, vol. 15, no. 9, pp. 953-957.
16. Cai, J. and Liu, Z., 1999. Integration of structural and statistical information for unconstrained handwritten Numeral Recognition. IEEE Transactions on Pattern Analysis and Machine Intelligence, vol. 21, no. 3, pp. 263-270.
17. Carbonnel, S. and Anquetil, E., 2004. Lexicon organization and string edit distance learning for lexical post-processing in handwriting recognition. Proceedings of IWFHR, pp. 462-467.
18. Casey, R. G. and Lecolinet, E., 1996. A survey of methods and strategies in character segmentation. IEEE Transactions on Pattern Analysis and Machine Intelligence, vol. 18, no. 7, pp. 690-706.
19. Chan, K. F. and Yeung, D. Y. 1999. Recognizing on-line handwritten alphanumeric characters through flexible structural matching. Pattern Recognition, vol. 32, no. 7, pp. 1099-1114.
20. Chang, C., 1994. Word class discovery for post-processing Chinese handwriting recognition. Proceedings of the 15th Conference on Computational Linguistics, vol.2, pp. 1221-1225.
21. Cho, S. and Kim, J. H., 2003. Bayesian network modeling of Hangul characters for on-line handwriting recognition. Proceedings of International Conference on Document Analysis and Recognition, pp. 207-211.
22. Cho, S., 1997. Neural-network classifiers for recognizing totally unconstrained handwritten numerals. IEEE Transactions on Neural Networks, vol. 8, no. 1, pp. 43-53.

23. Choi, M. and Kim, W., 2002. A novel two stage template matching method for rotation and illumination invariance. Pattern Recognition, vol. 35, no. 1, pp. 119-129.
24. Connell, S. D. and Jain A. K., 2001. Template-based online character recognition. Pattern Recognition, vol. 34, no. 1, pp. 1-14.
25. Connell, S. D. and Jain, A. K., 2002. Writer adaptation for online handwriting recognition. IEEE Transactions on Pattern Analysis and Machine Intelligence, vol. 24, no. 3, pp. 329-346.
26. Connell, S. D., Sinha, R. M. K. and Jain, A. K., 2000. Recognition of unconstrained online Devanagari characters. Proceedings of International Conference on Pattern Recognition, vol. 2, pp. 368-371.
27. Duneau, L. and Dorizzi, B., 1994. Online cursive script recognition: a system that adapts to an unknown user. Proceedings of International Conference on Pattern Recognition, vol. 2, pp. 24-28.
28. Elanwar, R. I., Rashwan, M. A., Mashali, S. A., 2007. Simultaneous segmentation and recognition of Arabic characters in an unconstrained online cursive handwritten document. Proceedings of World Academy of Science, Engineering and Technology, vol. 23, pp. 288-291.
29. Elnagar, A. and Alhajj, R., 2003. Segmentation of connected handwritten numeral strings. Pattern Recognition, vol. 36, no. 3, pp. 625-634.
30. Fitzgerald, J. A., Geiselbrechtinger, F., and Kechadi, T. 2004. Application of fuzzy logic to online recognition of handwritten symbols. Proceedings of the Ninth International Workshop on Frontiers in Handwriting Recognition, pp. 395-400.
31. Flusser, J., Boldy, J. and Zitova, B., 2003. Moment forms invariant to rotation and blur in arbitrary number of dimensions. IEEE Transactions on Pattern Analysis and Machine Intelligence, vol. 25, no. 2. pp. 234-245.
32. Freeman, H., 1974. Computer processing of line-drawing images. Computing Surveys, vol. 6, no. 1, pp. 57-97.
33. Fujimoto, Y., Kadota, S., Hayashi, S. and Yamamoto, M., 1976. Recognition of hand printed characters by nonlinear elastic matching. Proceedings of the Third Joint Conference on Pattern Recognition, pp. 113-118.

34. Funanda, A., Muramatsu, D., Matsumoto, T., 2004. The reduction of memory and the improvement of recognition rate for HMM on-line handwriting recognition. Proceedings of IWFHR, pp. 383-388.
35. Gader, P. D. and Khabou, M.A., 1996. Automatic feature generation for handwritten digit recognition. IEEE Transactions on Pattern Analysis and Machine Intelligence, vol. 18, no. 12, pp. 1256-1261.
36. Govindaraju, V., Srihari, S. N., 1997. Paradigms in handwriting recognition. Proceedings of IEEE International Conference on Systems, Man, and Cybernetics, pp. 1498 - 1503.
37. Guerfali, W and Plamondon, R, 1993. Normalizing and restoring online handwriting. Pattern Recognition, vol. 26, no. 3, pp. 419.
38. Guillevic, D. and Suen, C. Y., 1994. Cursive script recognition- a sentence level recognition scheme. Proceedings of IWFHR, pp. 216-223.
39. Gunter, S. and Bunke, H., 2004. Combination of three classifiers with different architectures for handwritten word recognition. Proceedings of IWFHR, pp. 63-68.
40. Guyon, I., Henderson, D., Albrecht, P., LeCun, Y. and Denker, J., 1992. Writer independent and writer adaptive neural network for on-line character recognition. In S. Impedovo and J. C. Simon (Eds.), From Pixels to Features. III: Frontiers in Handwriting Recognition, pp. 493-506.
41. Hartelius, K. and Carstensen, J. M., 2003. Bayesian grid matching. IEEE Transactions on Pattern Analysis and Machine Intelligence, vol. 25, no. 2, pp. 162-173.
42. Hseih, P., Wang, D. and Hsu, C., 2006. A linear feature extraction for multiclass classification problems based on class mean and covariance discriminant information. IEEE Transactions on Pattern Analysis and Machine Intelligence, vol. 28, no. 2, pp. 223-235.
43. Hu, J., Brown, M. K. and Turin, W., 1996. HMM based on-line handwriting recognition. IEEE Transactions on Pattern Analysis and Machine Intelligence, vol. 18, no. 10, pp. 1039-1045.
44. Hu, J., Lim, S. G. and Brown, M. K., 2000. Writer independent on-line handwriting recognition using an HMM approach. Pattern Recognition, vol. 33, no. 1, pp. 133-147.

45. Hu, J., Rosenthal, A. S. and Brown, M. K., 1997. Combining high level features with Sequential local features for online handwriting recognition. Proceedings of Italian Image Process conference, pp. 647-657.
46. Jaeger, S., Liu, L. C., Nakagawa, M., 2003. The state of art in Japanese online handwriting recognition compared to techniques in western handwriting recognition. International Journal of Document Analysis and Recognition, vol. 6, no. 2, pp. 75-88.
47. Jaeger, S., Manke, S., Reichert, J., Waibel A., 2001. Online handwriting recognition: the Npen++ Recognizer. International Journal of Document Analysis and Recognition, vol. 3, no. 3, pp. 169-180.
48. Jain, A. K and R. C. Dubes, 1988. Algorithms for clustering data. Prentice-Hall.
49. Jain, A. K., Duin, R.P.W. and Mao, J., 2000. Statistical pattern recognition: a review. IEEE Transactions on Pattern Analysis and Machine Intelligence, vol. 22, no. 1.pp. 4-37.
50. Jiang, Y., Ding, X., and Ren, Z. 2006. Substring alignment method for lexicon based handwritten chinese string recognition and its application to address line recognition. Proceedings of the 18th International Conference on Pattern Recognition, vol. 2, pp. 683-686.
51. Jung, K. and Kim, H. J., 2000. Online recognition of cursive Korean characters using graph representation. Pattern Recognition, vol. 33, pp. 399-412.
52. Kavallieratou, E., Fakatakis, N., Kolkkinakis, G., 2002. An unconstrained handwriting recognition system. International Journal of Document Analysis and Recognition, vol. 4, no. 4, pp. 226-242.
53. Kim, G. and Govindaraju, V., 1997. A lexicon driven approach to handwritten word recognition for real-time applications. IEEE Transactions on Pattern Analysis and Machine Intelligence, vol. 19, no. 4, pp. 366-379.
54. Kim, H. Y. and Kim, J. H., 2001. Hierarchical random graph representation of handwritten character and its application to Hangul recognition. Pattern Recognition, vol. 34, no. 2, pp. 187-201.
55. Kim, H. J., Kim, K. H., Kim, S. K., Lee, J. K., 1997. Online recognition of handwritten Chinese characters based on hidden markov models. Pattern Recognition, vol. 30, no. 9, pp. 1489-1500.

56. Kimura, Y., Wakahara, T. and Odaka, K., 1997. Combining statistical pattern recognition approach with neural networks for recognition of large-set categories. Proceedings of International Conference on Neural Networks, vol. 3, pp. 1429-1432.

57. Kobayashi, M., Masaki, S., Miyamoto, O., Nakagawa, Y., Komiya, Y. and Matsumoto, T., 2001. RAV (reparametrized angle variations) algorithm for online handwriting Recognition. International Journal of Document Analysis and Recognition, vol. 3, no. 1, 181-191.

58. Kuklinski, T. T., 1984. Components of handprint style variability. Proceedings of Seventh International Conference of Pattern Recognition, pp. 924-926.

59. Kurtzberg, J. M., 1987. Feature analysis for symbol recognition by elastic matching. IBM Journal of Research and Development, vol. 31, no. 1, pp. 91-95.

60. LeCun, Y. and Bengio, Y., 1994. Word-level training of handwritten word recognizer based on convolutional neural networks. Proceedings of International Conference on Pattern Recognition, vol. 2, pp. 88-92.

61. Lee, S., 1996. Off-line recognition of totally unconstrained handwritten numerals using multilayer cluster neural network. IEEE Transactions on Pattern Analysis and Machine Intelligence, vol. 18, no. 6, pp. 648-652.

62. Li, X. and Yeung, D. Y., 1997. Online handwritten alphanumeric character recognition using dominant points in strokes. Pattern Recognition, vol. 30, no. 1, pp. 31-44.

63. Liang, Z. and Shi, P., 2005. A metasynthetic approach for segmenting handwritten Chinese character strings. Pattern Recognition Letters, vol. 26, no. 10, pp. 1498-1511.

64. Lu, C. C. and Dunham, J. G., 1991. Highly efficient coding schemes for contour lines based on chain code representations. IEEE Transactions on Communications, vol. 39, no. 10, pp. 1511-1514.

65. Lu, Y. and Shridhar, M., 1996. Character segmentation in handwritten words – an overview. Pattern Recognition, vol. 29, pp. 77-96.

66. Ma, Y. and Leedham, G., 2007. Online recognition of handwritten Renqun shorthand for fast mobile Chinese text entry. Pattern Recognition Letters, vol. 28, no. 7, pp. 873-883.

67. Madhvanath, S., Kim, G., and Govindaraju, V. 1999. Chain code contour processing for handwritten word recognition. IEEE Transactions on Pattern Analysis and Machine Intelligence, vol. 21, no. 9, pp. 928-932.
68. Matic, N., Guyon, I. and Vapnik, V., 1993. Writer-adaptation for online handwritten character recognition. Proceedings of International Conference on Pattern Recognition and Document Analysis, pp. 187-191.
69. Mezghani, M., Cheriet, M. and Mitiche, A., 2003. Combination of pruned kohonen maps for online Arabic characters recognition. Proceedings of International Conference on Document Analysis and Recognition, pp. 900-904.
70. Morasso, P. G., Limoncelli, M. and Morchio, M., 1995. Incremental learning experiments with SCRIPTOR: an engine for online recognition of cursive handwriting. Machine Vision and Applications, 8, pp. 206-314.
71. Mozayyani, N., Baig, A. and Vaucher, G., 1998. A fully-neural solution for online handwritten character recognition. Proceedings of International Joint Conference on Neural Networks, vol. 2, pp. 160-164.
72. Nagy, G., 2000. Twenty years of document image analysis in pattern analysis and machine intelligence, IEEE Transactions on Pattern Analysis and Machine Intelligence, vol. 22, no. 1, pp. 38-62.
73. Nakai, M., Akira, N., Shimodiara, H., Sagayama, S., 2001. Substroke approach to hmm-based online Kanji handwriting recognition. Proceedings of International Conference on Document Analysis and Recognition, pp. 491-495.
74. Nathan, K. S., Subrahmonia, J. and Peronne, M. P., 1996. Parameter tying in writer dependent recognition of online handwriting. Proceedings of International Conference on Pattern Recognition, pp. 28-32.
75. Negi, A., Swaroop, K. S., Agarwal, A., 1995. A correspondence based approach to segmentation of cursive words. Proceedings of International Conference on Document Analysis and Recognition, pp. 1034-1037.
76. Nicchiotti, G. and Scagliola, C., 2000. A simple and effective cursive word segmentation method. Proceedings of the Seventh International Workshop on Frontiers of Handwriting Recognition, pp. 499-504.
77. Nouboud, F. and Plamondon, R., 1991. A structural approach to online character recognition: System design and applications. International Journal of Pattern Recognition and Artificial Intelligence, vol. 5, no. 1/2, pp. 311-335.

78. Oliveira, L. S., Sabourin, R., 2004. Support vector machines for handwritten numerical string recognition. Proceedings of ICFHR, pp. 39-44.
79. Paul, R., Nasif, M. S. and Farhad, S. M., 2007. Fingerprint recognition by chain coded string matching technique. Proceedings of International Conference on Information and Communication Technology, pp. 64-67.
80. Pavlidis, I., Singh, R. and Papanikolopoulos, N. P., 1997. An online handwritten note recognition method using shape metamorphosis. Proceedings of fifth International Conference on Document Analysis and Recognition, vol. 2, pp. 914-918.
81. Peng, H., Long, F. and Chi, Z., 2003. Document image recognition based on template matching of component block projections. IEEE Transactions on Pattern Analysis and Machine Intelligence, vol. 25, no. 9. pp. 1188-1192.
82. Pitrelli, J.F. and Perrone, M.P., 2002. Confidence modeling for verification post-processing for handwriting recognition. Proceedings of IWFHR, pp. 30-35.
83. Plamondon, R. and Srihari, S. N., 2000. Online and offline handwriting recognition: A comprehensive survey. IEEE Transactions on Pattern Analysis and Machine Intelligence, vol. 22, no. 1, pp. 63-84.
84. Prevost, L. and Milgram, M., 1997. Static and dynamic classifier fusion for character recognition. In Proceedings of fifth International Conference on Document Analysis and Recognition, vol. 2, pp. 499-506.
85. Rabiner, L. R., 1989. A tutorial on hidden Markov models and selected applications in speech recognition. Proceedings of IEEE, vol. 77, no. 2, pp. 257-286.
86. Ragot, N. and Anquetil, E., 2003. A generic hybrid classifier based on hierarchical fuzzy modeling: experiments on online handwritten character recognition. Proceedings of International Conference on Document Analysis and Recognition, pp. 963-967.
87. Rigoll, G., Kosmala, A., Rottland, J. and Neukirchen, C., 1996. A comparison between continuous and discrete density hidden Markov models for cursive handwriting recognition. Proceedings of International Conference on Pattern Recognition, vol. 2, pp. 205-209.
88. Rocha, J. and Pavlidis, T., 1994. A shape analysis model with applications to a character recognition system. IEEE Transactions on Pattern Analysis and Machine Intelligence, vol. 16, no. 4, pp. 393-404.

89. Ross, A., Dass, S. and Jain, A. K., 2005. A deformable model for fingerprint matching. Pattern Recognition, vol. 38, no. 1, pp. 95-103.
90. Sadri, J., Suen, C. Y. and Bui, T. D., 2007. A genetic framework using contextual knowledge for segmentation and recognition of handwritten numeral strings. Pattern Recognition, vol. 40, no. 3, pp. 898-919.
91. Scattolin, P., 1995, Recognition of handwritten numerals using elastic matching, Master's thesis, Concordia University, Canada.
92. Schenkel, M., Guyon, I. and Henderson, D., 1995. Online cursive script recognition using time-delay neural networks and hidden Markov models. Machine Vision and Applications, vol. 8, no. 4, pp. 215-223.
93. Schomaker, L., 1993. Using stroke or character based self-organizing maps in the recognition of online, connected cursive script. Pattern Recognition, vol. 26, no. 3, pp. 443-450.
94. Schplachbach, A. and Bunke, H., 2004. Using HMM based recognizers for writer identification and verification. Proceedings of IWFHR, pp. 167-172.
95. Schplachbach, A. and Bunke, H., 2007. Fusing asynchronous feature streams for on-line writer identification. Proceedings of International Conference on Document Analysis and Recognition, pp. 1-5.
96. Senior, A. and Nathan, K., 1997. Writer adaptation of a HMM handwriting recognition system. Proceedings of International Conference on Acoustics, Speech, and Signal Processing, vol. 2, pp. 1447-1450.
97. Shimodaira, H., Sudo, T., Nakai, M., Sagayama, S., 2003. Online overlaid-handwriting recognition based on substroke HMMs. Proceedings of International Conference on Document Analysis and Recognition, pp. 1043-1047.
98. Shin, J., 2004. Online cursive hangul recognition that uses DP matching to detect key segmentation points. Pattern Recognition, vol. 37, no. 11, pp. 2101-2112.
99. Shintani, H., Akutagawa, M., Nagashino, H., Kinouchi, Y., 2005. Recognition mechanism of a neural network for character recognition. Proceedings of Engineering in Medicine and Biology 27th Annual Conference, pp. 6540-6543.
100. Simoncini, L., Kovacs, M., 1995. A system for reading USA Census 90 handwritten fields. Proceedings of International Conference on Document Analysis and Recognition, vol. 2, pp. 86-91.

101. Slavik, P., Govindaraju, V., 2001. Equivalence of different methods for slant and skew corrections in word recognition applications. IEEE Transactions on Pattern Analysis and Machine Intelligence, vol. 23, no. 3, pp. 323-326.

102. Spitz, A.L., 1999. Shape-based word recognition. International Journal of Document Analysis and Recognition, vol. 1, pp. 178-190.

103. Stefano, L.D., Mattoccia, S. and Tombari, F., 2005. ZNCC-based template matching using bounded partial correlation. Pattern Recognition Letters, vol. 26, no. 14, pp. 2129-2134.

104. Subrahmonia, J., 2000. Similarity measures for writer clustering. In L. R. B. Schomaker and L. G. Vuurpijl (Eds.). Proceedings of the Seventh International Workshop on Frontiers in Handwriting Recognition, pp. 541-546.

105. Subrahmonia, J., Zimmerman, T., 2000. Pen computing: challenges and applications. Proceedings of 15th International Conference on Pattern Recognition, vol. 2, pp. 60-66.

106. Suen, C. Y., Koerich, A. L. and Sabourin, R., 2003. Lexicon-Driven HMM decoding for large vocabulary handwriting recognition with multiple character models. International Journal of Document Analysis and Recognition, vol 6, no. 2, pp. 126-144.

107. Tao, Yu, Muthukkumarasamy, V., Verma, B. and Blumenstein, M., 2003. A texture extraction technique using 2d-dft and hamming distance. Proceedings of fifth International Conference on Computational Intelligence and Multimedia Applications, pp. 120-125.

108. Tappert, C. C., 1982, Cursive script recognition by elastic matching. IBM Journal of Research and Development, vol. 26, no. 6, pp. 765-771.

109. Tappert, C. C., 1991. Speed, accuracy, and flexibility trade-offs in online character recognition. International Journal of Pattern Recognition and Artificial Intelligence, vol. 5, No. 1/2, pp. 79-95,

110. Tappert, C. C, 1984. Adaptive online handwriting recognition. Proceedings of International Conference of Pattern Recognition, pp. 1004-1007.

111. Tappert, C. C., Suen, C. Y., Wakahara, T., 1990. The state of the art in online handwriting recognition. IEEE Transactions on Pattern Analysis and Machine Intelligence, vol. 12, no. 8, pp. 787-808.

112. Tier, O. D, Jain, A. K. and Taxt, T., 1997. Feature extraction methods for character recognition - a survey. Pattern Recognition, vol. 29, no. 4, pp. 641-662.

113. Uchida, S. and Sakoe, H., 2005. A survey of elastic matching techniques for handwritten character recognition. IEICE Trans. Information and Systems, volE88-D, no. 8, pp. 1781-1790.
114. Uchida, S., Taira, E., Sakoe, H., 2001. Nonuniform slant correction using dynamic programming. Proceedings of International Conference on Document Analysis and Recognition. pp. 434-438.
115. Ueda, N. and Suzuki, S., 1990. Automatic shape model acquisition using multiscale segment matching. Proceedings of International Conference on Pattern Recognition, pp. 897-902.
116. Ueda, N. and Suzuki, S., 1993. Learning visual models from shape contours using multiscale convex/ concave structure matching. IEEE Transaction on Pattern Analysis and Machine Intelligence, vol. 15, no. 4, 337-352.
117. Unser, M., Aldroubi, A., Eden, M., 1993. B-Spline signal processing: part II - efficient design and applications. IEEE Transactions on Signal Processing, vol. 41, no. 2, pp. 834-848.
118. Veltman, S. R. and Prasad, R., 1994. Hidden markov models applied to online handwritten isolated character recognition. IEEE Transactions on Image Processing, vol. 3, no. 3, pp. 314-318.
119. Verma, B., Blumenstein, M., Ghosh, M., 2004. A novel approach for structural feature extraction: Contour vs. direction. Pattern Recognition Letters, vol. 25, no. 9, pp. 975-988.
120. Wakahara, T. and Odaka, K., 1997. Online cursive kanji character recognition using stroke-based affline transformation. IEEE Transactions on Pattern Analysis and Machine Intelligence, vol. 19, no. 12, pp. 1381-1385.
121. Wakahara, T., Murase, H., Odaka, K., 1992. Online handwriting recognition. Proceedings of IEEE, vol. 80, no. 7, pp. 1181-1194.
122. Ward, J. R. and Kuklinski, T., 1988. A model for variability effects in handprinting with implications for design of handwriting character recognition systems. IEEE Transactions on Systems, Man, and Cybernetics, vol 18, no, 3, pp. 438-451.
123. Webster, R. G. and Nakagawa, M., 1998. An interface-oriented approach to character recognition based on a dynamical model. Pattern Recognition, vol. 31, no. 2, pp. 193-203.

124. Wilfong, G., Sinden, F. and Ruedisueli, L., 1996. Online recognition of handwritten symbols. IEEE Transactions on Pattern Analysis and Machine Intelligence, vol. 18, no. 9, pp. 935-940.

125. Wing, A. M., 1979. Variability in handwritten characters. Visible Language, vol. 13, no. 3, pp. 283-298.

126. Yaeger, L. S., Webb, B. J. and Lyon, R. F., 1998. Combining neural networks and context-driven search for online, printed handwriting recognition in the NEWTON. AAAI's AI Magazine, vol. 19, no. 1, pp. 73-89.

127. Yamany, S. M. and Farag, A., 2002. Surface signatures: an orientation independent free-form surface representation scheme for the purpose of objects registration and matching. IEEE Transactions on Pattern Analysis and Machine Intelligence, vol. 24, no. 8, pp. 1105-1120.

128. Yang, D., Jin, L., Huo, Q., and He, T., 2007. Kernel modified quadratic discriminant function for online handwritten chinese characters recognition. Proceedings of the ninth International Conference on Document Analysis and Recognition, vol. 1, pp. 38-42.

129. Yanikoglu, B. and Sandon, P. A., 1998. Segmentation of off-line cursive handwriting using linear programming. Pattern Recognition, vol. 31, pp. 1825-1833.

130. Yimei, D., Fumitika, K., Yasuji, M., Malayappan, S., 2000. Slant estimation for handwritten words by directionally refined chain code. Proceedings of the Seventh International Workshop on Frontiers in Handwriting Recognition, pp. 53-62.

131. Yoshimura, I. and Yoshimura, M., 1992. Online signature verification incorporating the direction of pen movement – An experimental examination of the effectiveness. In from pixels to features III, International Workshop on Frontiers in Handwriting Recognition, pp 353-362.

132. Yuen, H., 1996. A chain coding approach for real-time recognition of online handwritten characters. Proceedings of International Conference on Acoustics, Speech, and Signal Processing, vol. 6, pp. 3426-3429.

133. Zanuy, M. F., 2007. Online signature recognition based on VQ-DTW. Pattern Recognition, vol. 40, no. 3, pp. 981-992.

134. Zhang, K., Pratikakis, I., Cornelis, J. and Nyssen, E., 2000. Using landmarks to establish a point-to-point correspondence between signatures. Pattern Analysis and Applications, vol. 3, no. 1, pp. 69-75.

135. Zheng, L., Hassin, A. H. and Tang, X., 2004. A new algorithm for machine printed Arabic character segmentation. Pattern Recognition Letters, vol. 25, no. 15, pp. 1723-1729.
136. Zhou, J., Gan, Q., Krzyzak, K., Suen, C. Y, 1999. Recognition of handwritten numerals by quantum neural network with fuzzy features. International Journal of Document Analysis and Recognition, vol. 2, pp. 30-36.

ABOUT THE AUTHOR

Dr. Anuj Sharma is PhD in computer science in the field of Pattern Recognition and Machine Learning. He has developed an Online Handwriting Recognizer as HWRAnuj and this book is an effort to present the digital handwriting interface of digital handwriting. He has written research papers in the field of Pattern Recognition and Machine Learning. He has done Post Doctoral fellowship from Germany. Presently, he is working as Assistant Professor in Panjab University, Chanigarh, India. Please find his updates at `sites.google.com/site/anujsharma25`